London Midland Region

David C. Williams

Ian Allan
PUBLISHING

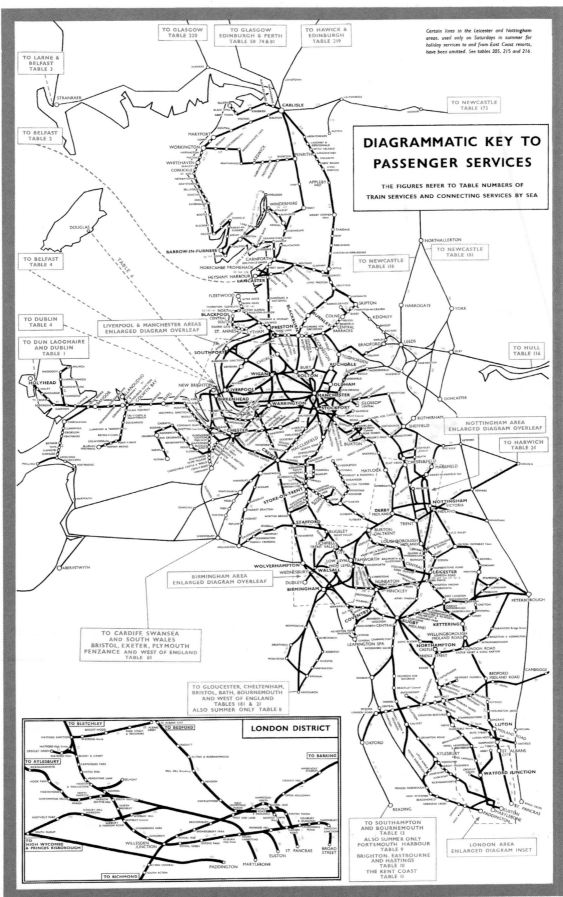

DIAGRAMMATIC KEY TO PASSENGER SERVICES

THE FIGURES REFER TO TABLE NUMBERS OF TRAIN SERVICES AND CONNECTING SERVICES BY SEA

Certain lines in the Leicester and Nottingham areas, used only on Saturdays in summer for holiday services to and from East Coast resorts, have been omitted. See tables 205, 215 and 216.

LONDON DISTRICT

BR. 86601/9   Printed by Stafford & Co., Ltd., Netherfield, Nottingham ( )

Front Cover: In the last few years of their operation, steam locomotives could still provide performances worthy of their youth. Here, Stanier Class 5 4-6-0 No 45455 of Carlisle Kingmore depot is vigorously addressing the four miles of 1 in 75 from Tebay to Shap summit above Scount Green with the Blackpool to Glasgow summer only train on Saturday 16 July 1966. No banking assistance is being provided for this 11 coach formation of BR standard coaches, weighing some 400 tons loaded, up one of the most severe main line gradients in Britain.

Title page: During the late afternoon of Saturday, 18 August 1962, LMS Hughes-designed, Horwich-built Class 5 'Crab' 2-6-0 No 42718 is being 'gassed up' for duty at Lancaster Green Ayre motive power depot alongside a dirtier classmate. The engine is based at Lower Darwen depot near Blackburn, and likely will be visiting the harbour/industrial complex at nearby Heysham to head a freight train home. Some 245 of these capable workhorses were built, No 42718 in 1927. The shed forming the backdrop closed in 1966; the Midland Railway through route from Wennington to Morecambe, which gave rise to most of the shed's business, closed completely one year later.

Left: A view from the footplate of a very work-stained 'Jubilee' Class 6P 4-6-0, No 45593 *Kolhapur* of Leeds Holbeck depot, heading the 06.17 Leeds City to Morecambe Promenade passenger train on the climb from Giggleswick to Eldroth summit, North Yorkshire, on Saturday, 15 May 1965. The ride was rough, but the engine was steaming extremely well; this was, to all enginemen, the most important factor – getting home! And the sound of this 'Jubilee' working hard remains memorable more than 40 years later.

FOREWORD

The compilation of this album has been a pleasurable experience. It has enabled me to recall, hopefully accurately, my activities over the last 12 years of steam on the London Midland Region.

The inspiration for doing it involves a little name-dropping. In my time as Severn Valley Railway chairman, magazine editor and locomotive driver, I had the good fortune to entertain on the Railway those most distinguished British railway photographers Eric Treacy and Bill Anderson, and also the prolific author and historian O.S. Nock. All were sadly in their declining years when I met them, but they all offered words of encouragement to me to produce for a wider public an album or two of steam photographs based on the selection that they saw.

I cannot claim that all, indeed any, of the chosen pictures are masterpieces, but I was 'out and about' amongst steam in the last decade, a 'new boy on the block' as far as they were concerned.

My hope is that this selection evokes happy memories for those active steam watchers at the time, and somehow conveys something of the great atmosphere of the 1960s steam railway system to those not lucky enough to have witnessed it first hand.

The photographs were all taken by me, except for two each by Michael York, and Lyn Whitworth. The captions and text are all my own work, and must therefore remain my responsibility. However, after 40 years, the memory can play tricks, and I would be pleased to receive comments and corrections via the publisher.

CONTENTS

First published 2008

ISBN 978 0 7110 3179 1

© David C. Williams 2008

Published by Ian Allan Publishing

an imprint of Ian Allan Publishing Ltd, Hersham, Surrey KT12 4RG

Printed in England by Ian Allan Printing Ltd, Hersham, Surrey KT12 4RG.

Code: 0806/B

Visit the Ian Allan Publishing website at www.ianallanpublishing.com

INTRODUCTION

The Demise of London Midland Steam

When Britain's railways were nationalised in 1948, the new organisation, entitled 'British Railways', inherited just over 20,000 steam locomotives. The territory and assets were divided amongst six Regions, the largest of which was the London Midland Region, basically the London, Midland & Scottish Railway in England and Wales, with nearly 10,000 steam locomotives. (Boundary adjustments were made later to tidy up the 'overlapping' with adjacent Regions in 'competing areas', but the London Midland remained the largest Region.)

Over the whole of British Railways, the rundown of steam power proceeded with vigour after nationalisation. Here are some of the causes:

1. Closure of hopelessly uneconomical routes, stations and facilities.
2. Elimination of competing routes of the pre-nationalisation companies.
3. Increases in road traffic and resultant decline in rail use, both passenger and freight, throughout the 1950s and 1960s.
4. The widespread introduction of diesel shunting locomotives from 1953 onwards.
5. Introduction of several electrification projects, such as Manchester-Sheffield-Wath in 1954.
6. Introduction of diesel multiple-units ('railcars') from 1954 onwards, their use becoming widespread from 1958 onwards.
7. The Modernisation Plan of 1955, resulting in introduction of main line diesel locomotives from 1959, becoming widespread from 1960 onwards.
8. The spread of West Coast electrification from 1960 onwards.

Above: This view was recorded at a location which became outside London Midland Region territory from 1958 onwards, but it is my only action shot of an important London Midland Region type still very active in the 1950s. When this was taken at Lansdowne Junction, Cheltenham, on Saturday, 30 April 1955, Gloucester Barnwood depot was home to no fewer than six veteran 'Midland Compound' Class 4P 4-4-0s; No 41195 is heading the 10.15am Gloucester Eastgate to Worcester Shrub Hill local formed of LMS Stanier stock. This engine was built at Derby in 1927, and scrapped there at the end of 1957, one of the last of 240 examples. The attractive red livery when built, and the visually slow revolution of their large 7ft diameter driving wheels earned them the nickname 'crimson ramblers'.

In those days, Lansdowne was a double junction, trains diverging for Kingham and Andover to the south, and Stratford to the north, both off the Birmingham to Bristol artery. Hence, within minutes of taking this picture, I had recorded Southern Class U 2-6-0 No 31626 and Great Western 4-6-0 No 6853 *Morehampton Grange* at this spot, representing three of the Big Four companies.

Each of the 'milestones' listed above saw localised groups of steam locomotives eliminated, but in 1962 and 1963, the trickle became a flood.

Unsurprisingly, with the major conurbations of London, the Midlands and North Western England all served intensively by steam-hauled freight traffic, the London Midland Region proved the most 'resistant' to the introduction of modern traction. It fell to the Liverpool, Manchester and Preston areas to draw the curtain down on British steam in August 1968, some 12 years before the most optimistic date envisaged in any of the various modernisation plans.

The London Midland fleet

In 1948, the locomotive design management team of the new national concern, British Railways, was mostly drawn from the staff of the London, Midland & Scottish Railway. This could easily be understood, for it was this company, more than any other, which had advanced the design of 'no frills' steam locomotives immediately before, and during World War 2. The evidence was provided by a fleet of 2,958 sturdy and reliable steam locomotives of 15 different designs that were built or rebuilt between 1933 and 1951. With one design exception, they steamed well, but all were a pleasure to drive and fire, and were sensible to maintain.

It is little wonder that these Stanier, Fairburn and Ivatt designs formed the basis for the range of 12 British Railways Riddles standard designs, a total of 999 examples of which were built between 1951 and 1960. But it should be added that they incorporated some of the best features from the three other Big Four companies, the Great Western, Southern and London & North Eastern Railways.

In addition to the 'modern' locomotives already mentioned, the London Midland Region was also operating a sizeable number of locomotives built to the designs of the LMS pre-1923 Grouping companies, many of the Midland

Above: A particularly long-serving locomotive series was the London & North Western Railway Class 6F and 7F 0-8-0 tender engines, known as 'Super Ds', represented here by '7F' No 48895 at Bescot on Sunday, 15 June 1963. Nominally, this Bowen-Cooke-designed, Crewe-built engine operated in freight service from 1904 until 1964, although how much of the original survived sixty years is open to some doubt! What is certain is that these engines gave yeoman service, and were much loved by management for their low operating costs. Some 572 LNWR 0-8-0s were built, although the early history is extremely complex, embracing different boilers, methods of propulsion and a host of detail variations. Some 442 of these engines entered BR service in 1948, and this one was the eldest of the last few extant in Black Country service at Bescot, near Walsall, West Midlands.

Railway-design examples actually having been built after the formation of the LMS. By comparison, the London & North Western Railway types were quickly 'extinguished' during the early 1950s, with the notable exception of the 0-8-0 freight tender engines. And the Lancashire & Yorkshire Railway locomotives were withdrawn slightly less earnestly, with 0-6-0 tender engines and some shunting and dock tanks also surviving into the early 1960s.

THE PERSONAL ANGLE

As a youngster, teenager and 'young chap', I was fortunate to have witnessed the final 20 years of steam traction in Britain.

Early on, most enthusiasts of the period little realised the significance of what they were recording; I, for one, really believed that steam would last for ever, with only new types replacing old! In this connection, I was very envious of older local enthusiasts such as the legendary W.A. Camwell – my parents' bank manager – who fondly recalled the 'Claughtons', 'Cauliflowers', 'Flatirons', and much else of an earlier era. And many of his contemporaries were actually contemptuous of such 'modern monstrosities' as the Class 9F 2-10-0s!

Arthur, my father, was an electrical engineer by profession, but was interested in all aspects of travel and engineering, including steam traction. He acquired his first car in 1951, and was soon using it to visit places of note from Land's End to John o'Groats, with my mother Gwen and myself in attendance. Railway viewing was on the agenda, together with a limited amount of photography; limited, I might add, by the availability of pocket money! For his part, my father boasted to work colleagues that he was acquainted with every road-over-rail bridge between Rugby and Crewe, and Banbury and Solihull. It is doubtful if they were very impressed!

Although achieved by road transport means, I had visited most of the far-flung and scenic parts of the BR system. However, I had spent little time actually aboard trains and had not experienced the industrial areas of the national network – and even less after my mother had been duped into spending an 'afternoon out' at the delightfully misnamed Rose Grove locomotive shed and station!

For me, the real opportunity for intensive watching and spotting presented itself with participation in Stephenson Locomotive Society railtours from 1958 onwards, and membership of the Birmingham Locospotters Club from 1960. Both of these organisations supplied budget-priced visits to railway installations that were usually 'off limits' to 16 year olds.

Although I had visited every major BR motive power depot by 1962, and indeed seen every extant BR locomotive by 1963, I was always as interested in the railway *ambience* as in the locospotting. The stations, depots and much of the

Above: On the sunny Sunday of 28 February 1960, red 'Duchess' Pacific No 46226 *Duchess of Norfolk* of Carlisle Upperby depot leads a 14-coach train of LMS stock downhill along the straight tangent from Penkridge to Stafford at Dunston, a pretty village on the southern edge of the county town. The train has been subject to diversion from the West Coast main line (WCML) because of engineering work and has travelled from Rugby via Coventry, Aston, Bescot and Bushbury – a real 'shed bash' for anyone travelling on this train!

infrastructure fascinated me; railway history and geography were absorbed through book purchases, and my minuscule but precious engineering apprenticeship wage was also used to purchase tickets for trains – hopefully steam-hauled – to interesting places around the system. Lineside photography, tape recording and the occasional footplate ride were the main aims.

In the last few years of operation, steam locomotives were neglected more than ever. I became one of a band of enthusiasts, from all walks of life and from all parts of Britain, who secured 'local' permission to clean, even partially repaint, steam locomotives during the night or early morning. We then photographed them on known duties during that and successive days.

In addition to cleaning and repainting, my own draughting background enabled me to produce replica smokebox numberplates for Western Region or standard engines when these items were missing. The plates were made to the correct style – I saw no point in making 'crude' replacements – with carefully cut and painted balsa wood numerals nailed to a correct size hardboard panel. We also had a few spare genuine shedplates to bolt onto smokebox doors if they were missing - such plates were only worth a few shillings in those days! No 75019 on the Grassington Branch (Page 87) is an example of the 'full treatment'.

I realise that this enthusiasm was beyond the normal call, and some would say probably verging on insanity! But people in their teens and twenties have boundless energy, and only after a 40-year interval am I admitting to some of these antics. Besides, during the intervening years, the demands of the developing Severn Valley Railway have taken up my time fully, and prevented a considered review. Until now, that is . . .

COVERAGE

Very few people covered all the areas of the London Midland Region photographically. In my case, there are strengths and weaknesses; there is a bias towards the Midlands and North West, because I have lived, worked and holidayed in these areas. The London area was neglected because, as a Midlander, the temptation of rushing to see Eastern and Southern Region locomotives in the metropolis was too great!

The last few years of steam operation in Britain attracted unprecedented attention from enthusiasts in words and pictures, and this turned into almost feverish activity as the end in 1968 approached. The purpose of this book is to highlight area-by-area the rundown of London Midland Region steam, with particular reference to ordinary day-to-day activities. Steam-hauled railtours for enthusiasts, with the locomotive festooned in headboards, are minimally shown, as are the usual horrors of dreadfully neglected locomotives wreathed in steam, leaking from every joint, with numberplates or nameplates missing or hanging off. That isn't steam power as I would like to remember it.

This is steam *towards* the end, not *at* the end.

ACKNOWLEDGEMENTS

Many of the photographs that appear in this book were only made possible through the willing and enthusiastic co-operation of railwaymen of all trades and grades. First of all, the management: I was fortunate to have been able to obtain lineside photographic passes for the London Midland Region Birmingham and Manchester areas. These enabled me to *officially* cross the lineside fences, always taking care, of course, to inform relevant signalmen, and others in charge, of my intended activities.

This leads me neatly to acknowledge that signalmen often provided vital information about train operations, and sometimes the odd 'cuppa' into the bargain – and very welcome it was, too!

Footplatemen also were key players in the success of my activities, hopefully providing suitable smoke effects if contactable and able, and allowing footplate visits and, best of all, in some cases unofficial footplate rides! (It should be mentioned, however, that steam locomotives were not supposed to smoke their way around the countryside – read the handbook.)

Above: The Stanier Class 8F 2-8-0s could justifiably be regarded as the backbone of London Midland long-distance freight operations from the mid-1930s onwards. Following distinguished war service in Europe and Asia for many of them, no fewer than 666 examples had reached British Railways stock by 1957. As could be expected, the bulk of this type was allocated to the London Midland Region, but some came under Western, Eastern, North Eastern and Scottish jurisdiction. On the pleasant autumn morning of Saturday, 16 October 1965, No 48339, a long-time resident of Saltley depot, Birmingham, completes a return trip to Bescot, near Walsall, along the Sutton Park line, joining the Derby to Birmingham main line here at Castle Bromwich Junction. The impressive smoke effect might have resulted from a 'go for it' gesture from the signalman at Park Lane Junction!

Locomotive sheds – motive power depots in official parlance – were usually worth a visit, particularly if most of the staff were of a friendly disposition. Shedmasters, or in their absence shift foremen, could sometimes be persuaded to permit unofficial visits – on occasion during the overnight period – and allowed specific locomotives to be cleaned by us, even partially repainted by us, to enable ourselves and many others to photograph a particular working a few hours later. It is safe to mention some of these LMR locations with the passage of time; Bescot, Birkenhead, Rose Grove, Buxton, Kingmoor, Carnforth, Lostock Hall and Patricroft. And the staff at Kendal goods yard provided facilities at this most unlikely venue for engine cleaning!

So, thanks are owed to the many railwaymen who 'enabled' all these activities to take place. It could only have happened in the 1960s; 10 years earlier, the management was rather more authoritarian, and 10 years later, collectively you needed to buy your own Railway to clean engines. So, some of us did just that!

After steam finished, and into Severn Valley Railway days, I got to know these London Midland footplatemen; Jack Beaman (Saltley and Aston), Ron Gardner (Saltley), the late Maurice Newman (Walsall Ryecroft and Saltley) and Lyn Whitworth (Saltley). All of them provided interesting and informative 'inside knowledge', often probably unknowingly, whilst they introduced me to 14 years of living on steam locomotive footplates at Bridgnorth and Bewdley.

Thanks!

David C. Williams
Shenstone, Lichfield, Staffordshire
27 August 2007

The headquarters of the London Midland Region was situated at Euston station in London, the site having performed a similar function previously for the London & Birmingham Railway, the London & North Western Railway and the London, Midland & Scottish Railway. Apart from the memorable Doric style archway which formed the main entrance, 1837-built and insensitively demolished in 1962, the station was neither as impressive as its counterparts at St Pancras, King's Cross and Paddington, nor as intimate as Marylebone. It was, however, very busy, and in the late 1950s dealt typically with nearly 100 ordinary main line departures and arrivals every day, augmented considerably by holiday and seasonal extras ('reliefs'). Euston also hosted inner and outer suburban activity. It was the only London station to serve England, Scotland, Wales and Ireland, both north and south, directly on a daily basis.

Steam traction was unchallenged at Euston from the station's inception until the suburban electrification of 1914. Steam continued to play a major role in powering all other services until the widespread introduction of main line diesel locomotives in 1959-62. Certain peripheral duties, including relief trains, parcels traffic, shunting and – not least – substitution for diesel failures, continued in a gradually diminishing fashion until 1965; soon after, overhead wires were energised, and a full electric locomotive-hauled main line service commenced in 1966.

Above: A deceptively quiet scene at one of the departure platforms, 12, as locally based 'Duchess' Pacific No 46239 *City of Chester* in green livery awaits departure with the 4.35pm train to Wolverhampton on Saturday, 24 August 1963. Camden had lost its handful of steam locomotives a few weeks previously, and now Willesden-based, No 46239 is at last receiving cleaning attention in the roundhouse there. *Michael York*

Right: On Thursday, 2 February 1959, Platform 1 sees the arrival of 'The Mancunian', the 9.40am from Manchester London Road to Euston nonstop train, behind 'Royal Scot' Class 7P 4-6-0 No 46137 *The Prince of Wales's Volunteers (South Lancashire)* of Manchester Longsight depot. The 'Royal Scots' formed the backbone of Euston express services for over 30 years, and this one was the last of the 71 engines to be converted from Fowler parallel boiler to Stanier taper boiler design with new cylinders, some four years before this view was recorded.

BLETCHLEY

Some 46 miles north of London Euston lies the important Buckinghamshire junction of Bletchley, where the West Coast main line bisects the cross-country Oxford to Cambridge route. In steam days, the latter was a strategically important passenger and freight link; the locomotive shed adjacent to the station entrance yard at Bletchley was always busy, servicing the motive power for various interchange freight activities, together with outer suburban and a few rural local passenger trains. The increase in road traffic, the rationalisation of railway freight services, and the modernisation of motive power all combined to bring about the closure of the steam depot in 1965, leaving establishments like this confined to history. Bletchley is now part of the New Town of Milton Keynes, and despite the massive population explosion, the only rural passenger route to survive here is the one to Bedford.

Sunday was a quiet day at most steam depots, particularly those that dealt predominantly with freight power. The silence was frequently broken, however, by the noise of shunting operations for the servicing and turning of locomotives for the start of the working week on Monday morning.

Left: Stanier 'Jubilee' Class 6P 4-6-0 No 45721 *Impregnable* of Crewe North is the shunt engine at Bletchley on 3 March 1963, and has already deposited Stanier '8P' Pacific No 46225 *Duchess of Gloucester* of Carlisle Upperby in the boundary siding.

Middle: 'Jubilee' No 45721 *Impregnable* is attempting to move locally-based Stanier Class 8F 2-8-0 No 48427 across the yard; with greasy rails, this was not always as easy to achieve as it might seem.

Below: No 46225 *Duchess of Gloucester,* in begrimed red livery, resides in its new location, which looks deceptively rural from this angle. These impressive engines were more commonly seen on Bletchley depot from 1960 onwards, after most of their main line duties were dieselised. Previously, only the occasional main line failure brought an '8P' appearance at Bletchley, and indeed on this occasion No 46220 *Coronation* was in residence deep in the depot after some 'trouble'.

Proceeding further north along the West Coast main line, at 82 miles from London, we arrive at the important railway centre of Rugby. The town of Rugby increased in importance with the opening of the London & Birmingham Railway in 1838, and within a few short years rail links with Stafford, Leamington, Northampton, Peterborough and Leicester set the seal on Rugby's status as the railway gateway to the Midlands from the south. This impression was reinforced by the presence of a huge locomotive depot situated on the Up side immediately south of the station, which opened on this site in 1876 and closed to steam in 1965.

Top: On Saturday, 11 May 1963, Stanier 'Jubilee' 4-6-0 No 45705 *Seahorse* of Newton Heath depot, Manchester, is making a minimum of fuss on the 1 in 200 climb out of Rugby, appropriately with a Rugby League Cup Final special train for London. The engine is smartly turned out for this rare trip to the capital. The threadbare embankment from which the photo was taken was a Mecca for enthusiasts. Most train movements could be seen, including crucially the activities on the Great Central main line within the 'birdcage' bridge above, which excitingly brought LNER main line power through the south and east Midlands.

Middle: 'Britannia' Pacific No 70018 *Flying Dutchman* of Crewe North depot heads a lengthy train of empty newspaper vans southwards under the Great Central 'birdcage' bridge at Rugby on 11 May 1963. Such a duty does not enjoy the status of the Cardiff to London and Carlisle to Edinburgh trains that the engine worked in the recent past.

Right: On Sunday, 8 September 1963, Camden's red 'Duchess' Pacific No 46245 *City of London* makes both a handsome and powerful sight at the south end of Rugby Midland station's Platform 2 at the business end of a London train. In the distance is the 'birdcage' bridge of the Great Central main line. A forest of overhead masts on the lower level and total closure of the higher level were very soon to transform this scene, but most of the 'birdcage' survived here until lifted away in January 2007.

The Trent Valley section of the West Coast main line opened in 1847, and effectively, four tracks have been available for trains from London to Tamworth, Staffordshire, some 110 miles distant, since 1901. At the minor road overbridge at Alvecote, north of Polesworth, North Warwickshire, we are still above the four-track section, two miles south of the Tamworth to Rugeley 'bottleneck', which is in course of elimination, with completion planned in 2009.

Above: Here is an engine with some racing pedigree, albeit under 1960s grime. Red Stanier 'Princess Royal' 4-6-2 No 46207 *Princess Arthur of Connaught* of Camden depot sweeps northwards on the Up Fast line on Saturday, 17 October 1959, with a diverse rake of coaches forming an unidentified express. The name of this engine always attracted lineside comment and curiosity, and to the aficionados, this was the one that had tragically rolled into a field at Weedon, Northamptonshire, some eight years previously. The land to the right of this view is adjacent to the 12th century Alvecote Priory, which attracted a steady stream of weekend visitors. However, my parents and I were the only ones visiting what seemed to us this equally, if not more, interesting attraction, the busy West Coast main line at Alvecote on that day!

Below: On 17 October 1959, a southbound express goods train, powered by Stanier Class 5 4-6-0 No 45381 of Willesden depot, speeds through Tamworth on the Up Fast line. In the background is Marshall's Sidings signalbox, controlling movements to and from the adjacent goods yard, and active from 1877 until 1962.

Above: An 'intimate' view of traffic on the Down Slow line at Tamworth was available from the steps of a footbridge, south of the road bridge, which did not survive the 1963 electrification. Long-time Nuneaton resident Stanier '8F' 2-8-0 No 48723 wheels a northbound pick-up goods on a turn that could produce a Bowen-Cooke 'Super D' 0-8-0, a Fowler '4F' 0-6-0 or a 2-6-0 of Hughes, Stanier or Ivatt ancestry, such was the train's status and timing allowance!

The first railway station in Birmingham was Curzon Street terminus, opened in 1839 by the London & Birmingham Railway, and soon used also by the Grand Junction Railway linking northwards to Manchester and Liverpool. A period of rapid rail network expansion followed, and Curzon Street soon proved to be badly sited and inadequate. Black Country interests saw the Stour Valley Railway of 1852 burst under the city in a long tunnel, providing a more direct link to Wolverhampton and creating a through route from London to the north. Thus the through station of New Street was born, and it officially opened in 1854. Curzon Street spent over a century in use as a parcels and mail depot, which ensured that the splendid building survived, unlike its opposite number at London Euston.

It is difficult to describe Birmingham New Street station in a few words. Indeed, it was really two stations situated alongside each other, separated by a sett-surfaced roadway known as Queen's Drive. Both stations gave open access to the public, who could thus wander around everywhere on the site at will. The north side of the area, nearest to the city centre, was occupied by the North Western station, which served London to Wolverhampton, Crewe and the northwest of England. The south side of the site contained the Midland station, serving the route from the northeast of England and Sheffield to Bristol and the southwest. All of this supported New Street's claim to be the busiest *main line* station in Britain. World War 2 bombing had completely decimated the North Western overall roof, which was not replaced and allowed direct sun penetration, as these views show. The roof of the Midland side of the station was repaired, and views within it are shown later in this book.

Right: Harsh weather early in 1965 contributed to a shortage of diesel multiple-unit trains in the Birmingham area, and a few rush hour local trains to a variety of destinations reverted to locomotive haulage by steam or diesel power. Most were hauled by Stanier Class 5 locomotives, with, sensationally, a few 'Britannia' Pacifics involved. The main attraction to local enthusiasts, however, was the reallocation of four Fairburn Class 4 2-6-4 tanks from Stoke to Aston, three of which were used; these and other steam appeared on the Aston-Sutton Coldfield-Lichfield line for the first time in nine years. Recalling past pleasures, No 42075 awaits departure time, in this case with the 17.40 train to Walsall on Wednesday, 3 March 1965.

Below: Platform 1 is where 'it all happened', the usual departure point for London trains. This, however, is an important exception; it is the 10.55am to Glasgow, which often brought Class 7P 'Royal Scot' power to Birmingham. (In that pre-diesel period, Class 6P 'Jubilees' and 'Patriots' were the common currency at both sides of New Street rather than '7Ps.') The unique 'Royal Scot' 4-6-0 No 46170 *British Legion* of Crewe North is in attendance, on 28 March 1959. Drivers agreed that No 46170 was a 'rough old nag', so the 53-mile run home was an appropriately less-taxing assignment on this occasion. Certainly, nobody seemed to mind 'losing' the engine deep in the back of Rugby shed for a month for the Remembrance service!

Here, the western end of New Street's North Western side is featured: a less popular place to view activity, but well liked on winter days because of the proximity of the very hospitable Platform 6 refreshment room!

At first, the introduction of BR Standard locomotives in the 1950s made very little difference to the motive power situation on the North Western side of Birmingham New Street. The LMS dominance persisted until the last few years of steam operations, when nearby Aston depot became swamped, first with Class 4 4-6-0s and then with 'Britannia' Pacifics.

Left: The almost universal employment of Stanier Class 5 4-6-0s on North Western section duties at Birmingham New Street was slightly reduced by the acquisition of six BR Standard Class 5 4-6-0s by London's Willesden depot in 1961-3, this group then moving to Bletchley and Nuneaton for another six months. No 73013 of Willesden (1A) depot stands in Platform 6 with an arrival from the south in 1962 or 1963.

Right: A late afternoon arrival at Platform 6, the 4.07pm from Bletchley, could turn up with almost any type of locomotive in charge, from BR Standard Class 4 2-6-4 tanks upwards. Here is shown the ultimate power on Saturday, 16 May 1964. Willesden-based Stanier Pacific No 46245 *City of London*, in immaculate red livery, has just completed the undemanding task, and its youthful fireman has instantly become the envy of an enlarging swarm of platform-end enthusiasts.

Left: Two frequently seen, but somehow relatively easily overlooked LMS locomotive types are here seen alongside. On the left, Caprotti valve gear-propelled Class 5 4-6-0 No 44748 of Longsight is at Platform 5, with Hughes 'Crab' 2-6-0 No 42859 of Willesden at Platform 6 with a parcels train. The trains concerned and the date, in 1959 or 1960, is unrecorded. More New Street scenes, on the Midland side, are shown on pages 58 and 59.

Two-and-a-half miles away from New Street along the Grand Junction route is the important and one-time triple junction of Aston, where lines to Stechford and Lichfield still diverge at opposite ends of the platform from the Birmingham to Bescot route. The short branch to Windsor Street goods depot and coal yard was closed in 1980, and is now lifted. With the locomotive depot also situated near to the station in the fork of the New Street and Stechford lines, the track layout was extremely cramped, and the elevated merely double-track section through the station was very busy at all times; indeed, it still is. This key location lay half-a-mile distant from my workplace for over eight years at the GEC factory at Witton. Now, nearly 50 years later, the memories of intensive steam activity at lunchtime mark a hectic but rewarding period of my life. Here are three 1960s views when the sun penetrated the smoky murk at Aston station.

Top: Stanier Class 8F 2-8-0 No 48335 from Bescot depot is in charge of a relatively lightweight train at Aston that nevertheless contains a valuable load of coal for Windsor Street early in 1962. A few years earlier, 0-8-0s and 0-6-0s had more usually performed this type of work, simply because 2-8-0s could not be spared from their main line assignments, such as the Toton (Nottingham) to Brent (North London) coal traffic.

Middle: Aston saw many locomotive changes during the last couple of years of steam traction, as budgets for operating steam were trimmed to pay for widespread dieselisation. The aim was generally to maximise the operation of any steam locomotive that possessed a long-term boiler expiry date and was in adequate mechanical order with no known large repair bills lurking. For instance, BR Standard Class 4 2-6-0s had not been commonly seen in the Birmingham area, but several were moved to Saltley following redundancy in London and Scotland, thanks in part to the efforts of driver and enthusiast the late Maurice Newman. Originally an Eastern Region engine, No 76040 became a Saltley engine and, in 1965, a loan example at Aston. Here, in the summer of 1965, it is arriving at Aston from Stechford with a local freight. Two years later, it was written off the books, a refurbished replacement 'Monitor' injector marked '76040' remaining in the stores at Saltley unused for several years after the demise of steam, let alone this engine!

Bottom: Towards the end of steam operations, most of the suitable suburban passenger work for tank engines had disappeared. A small number were retained for parcels traffic and the occasional diesel railcar substitution. This Stanier 2-6-4 tank, No 42573 of Rugby, is returning from a morning sortie to drop on to Aston shed, just a few yards ahead, in early 1962.

Top: Utilising my lineside permit, I exceeded my allotted lunch hour considerably by following another 'rare bird', ex Crosti-boilered 2-10-0 No 92029, newly homed at Saltley depot, down the Windsor Street goods branch. The driver proffered the information that the locomotive was in deplorable condition, but being a large beast, even the available 'half-power' provided a similar output to a Class 3F 0-6-0! Souvenir hunters had already 'rescued' the front numberplate before this date, Wednesday, 23 March 1966.

Middle: Stretching the validity of my local lineside permit somewhat (although I had the shedmaster's tacit approval), Aston shed yard was the occasional venue for lunchtime photographic activities. Here, the huge mechanical coaling plant forms the backdrop for Stanier Class 5 4-6-0 No 45369 of Saltley depot, early in 1964.

Below: Just over one mile from Aston on the Grand Junction (Bescot) line is Witton station, actually the closest to Aston Villa football ground and also quite near to my GEC place of work. Aside from match days, it was a quiet place, admirably suited to lunchtime train watching. This was a routine sight in the lunch hour, a Stanier Class 8F 2-8-0, in this case No 48662 of Burton depot, wheeling a lengthy freight from the north past the ICI Kynoch works offices at Witton in 1962.

Walsall station was of typical London & North Western Railway construction, with timber boarding virtually everywhere; but its location was distinctive, at the end of a short cut-and-cover tunnel under the town's main thoroughfare, Park Street, where the low-lying track was very susceptible to flooding. On this page, I have matched the gloom of Great Bridge on a dull winter's day with the gloom of Walsall station.

Top left: A visit to the steam scrapyard of John Cashmore at Great Bridge on Tuesday, 9 November 1965 was interrupted by the passage of Stanier Class 8F 2-8-0 No 48478 of Bescot depot heading for Dudley with a mixed freight. The location is the bridge over the Tame Valley canal on the approach to Eagle Crossing. With the withdrawal from service of 0-8-0s and 0-6-0s, the brunt of Black Country freight workings were shouldered by these capable machines for the last few years of steam working.

Top right: The 245 Hughes-designed 2-6-0s, universally nicknamed 'Crabs', performed useful mixed traffic duties over a large part of the LMS system. Typical of the work performed was parcels duty, and No 42782 of Bescot depot is so engaged in Walsall's parcels bay platform on Friday, 30 October 1959.

Below: The typical LNWR 'northlight' roof of Bushbury depot, Wolverhampton, bestrides a smoky interior on the Sunday morning of 2 March 1963. The dramatic rays of rising sun are catching the fresh paintwork of Leeds Farnley Junction 'Jubilee' 4-6-0 No 45581 *Bihar and Orissa*, rarely seen in these parts unless visiting Crewe Works as on this occasion.

SUTTON COLDFIELD

This area was my home for 40 years, and although two LMS routes crossed here, it has always been something of a railway 'backwater'. The two lines concerned are the London & North Western Railway Aston to Lichfield line, completed to Sutton in 1862 and extended to Lichfield in 1884, and the Midland Railway Castle Bromwich to Walsall Ryecroft route (the Sutton Park line) of 1879. Unfortunately for enthusiasts, the two lines crossed in an inaccessible location to the north of Sutton Coldfield town centre. Being at school in central Sutton from 1957 to 1961, and close to the activity for another five years, even the 'backwater' eventually yielded everything from an 'A3' 4-6-2 to Class 3F 0-6-0s on the Sutton Coldfield line, and 'Duchesses' to a Radstock Sentinel 0-4-0 on the Sutton Park line. (The latter, No 47190, ran hot and spent a few days at Sutton Park station in early March 1961.)

Left: The morning pick-up goods (166 trip), 10.40am from Lichfield City to Birmingham Curzon Street or Aston, was in my time worked by 'Super D' 0-8-0s, then Hughes or Stanier 2-6-0s, and finally Stanier '8F' 2-8-0s from Aston depot. One of the Aston quartet of 2-8-0s employed, No 48752 complete with Fowler tender, stands in Sutton Coldfield station on a warm day in June 1959. It is the school lunch hour, and my friend Tony Vass and I were allowed to drive the engine up and down the headshunt several times by a friendly Aston driver. What a way to spend lunchtime! No 48752 is standing more or less where 'Black Five' No 45274 had so tragically finished up, lying on its side after the rail crash some four years earlier.

Right: The Sutton Coldfield line passenger service went all diesel multiple-unit from March 1956 onwards, but some interest returned with the introduction of the summer overnight 'car sleeper' service to Stirling, Scotland, from June 1958. Ultimately, motive power could be 'Royal Scot', 'Jubilee', 'Patriot', 'Black Five', 'Britannia', 'Clan', '73xxx' or 'A3' engines, usually supplied by Leeds Holbeck, Carlisle Kingmoor or Aston depots. Here, 'Royal Scot' No 46162 *Queen's Westminster Rifleman* of Saltley depot reposes in Sutton's car sleeper platform at 7.30pm on, I believe, Sunday, 2 July 1961. (This is the original Sutton Coldfield terminus of 1862.) No 46162 will reverse the sleeping cars onto the 'main line', and bring them into the through platform beyond the wall. Then the shunt engine, often Stanier Class 3 2-6-2 tank No 40180, will add the car-carrying vans on to the rear of the train, and at 9.43pm the sound of the 'Scot' addressing the 1 in 100 climb to Four Oaks will be heard all over a restful Sutton Coldfield. Happy days!

Left: The centenary of the Sutton Coldfield line was celebrated on Saturday, 2 June 1962 by the operation of a Stephenson Locomotive Society special train from Birmingham New Street, hauled by one of Bescot's LNWR 'Super D' 0-8-0s, No 48930. This type had long been associated with both of Sutton's railways on freight work; only the Webb 0-6-2 'Coal tank' No 58926 would have been more appropriate, but was not active then. The 0-8-0 is seen leaving Sutton Coldfield on the return journey

Lichfield Trent Valley station was a Mecca for enthusiasts from all over the West Midlands, with easy rail access to the High Level station from two routes. It was a superb place to watch trains; Tamworth, although busier, was less accessible by rail from the Black Country, and the platforms were always 'out of bounds' to spotters, relegating them to a very poor viewpoint. Here is the main line at Lichfield Trent Valley, running through the Low Level platforms.

Right: Most trains traversing the Trent Valley section of the West Coast main line sped through Lichfield Trent Valley station on the centrally situated fast lines, but the occasional 'stopper' provided an opportunity to examine a main line locomotive at close quarters. The 12.00 noon from London Euston to Crewe called at most stations along the way, a real treat for any enthusiast-traveller with time to spare! Here, rebuilt 'Patriot' 4-6-0 No 45540 *Sir Robert Turnbull* of Manchester's Longsight depot (always recognisable by its widely spaced smokebox door numerals) arrives at Lichfield for a brief stop at 2.56pm.

Below: This is the magic moment when two giants pass, on Tuesday, 23 February 1960. Red 'Duchess' 4-6-2 No 46254 *City of Stoke-on-Trent* (one of only three with badges above the nameplates) on the Down 'Royal Scot', 10.00am from London Euston to Glasgow Central, meets 'Royal Scot' 4-6-0 No 46122 *Royal Ulster Rifleman*. The span of Burton Old Road bridge has been being lifted for impending electrification.

Here is more activity at Lichfield Trent Valley, at High Level, reflecting the everyday scene.

Top: Passing the extremely basic sleeper-boarded platforms of High Level, Stanier Class 8F 2-8-0 No 48514 labours uphill with a coal train from Wichnor Junction to Bescot yard on a misty day, Tuesday, 23 February 1960. This train was part of a frequent service (nowadays called a 'flow'!) that brought coal mined in the North and East Midlands for use in the industrial West Midlands. No 48514 was a long-time Bescot resident. In the background is the Streethay pumping station of the South Staffordshire Waterworks Company, whose buildings are invariably 'distinguished looking' in this area.

Middle: On a summer Saturday in 1956, Ivatt Class 2 2-6-2 tank No 41223 has just worked the 1.59pm from Walsall to Lichfield Trent Valley 'push-and-pull', and is 'laying over' in the loop north of Trent Valley High Level prior to returning to Lichfield City to work the 4.44pm to Walsall.

Bottom: Stanier Class 3 2-6-2 tank No 40207 of Bushbury, Wolverhampton, draws the stock of the 1.20pm from Birmingham New Street away from High Level to the run-round loop in the summer of 1955. In the background are the prominent buildings of Thomas & Evans Maltings.

Rugeley Trent Valley was a busy place to watch trains. Although situated a mile away from the town centre, so passenger trade wasn't as lucrative as it might have been, the place was popular with enthusiasts from the West Midlands area. The main line procession was supplemented by traffic from effectively three facing junctions – at Lichfield TV spur, Rugeley TV itself and Colwich – so it was quite busy.

North of Rugeley, the Trent Valley section of the West Coast main line comprises four tracks as far as Colwich Junction, two miles away, where the direct Stoke and Manchester line leaves the route to Crewe and the north, which threads Shugborough Tunnel before reaching Stafford. Bishton Lane overbridge, and a country lane running parallel on this section were favourite places to watch trains.

Right: The murky wet morning of Friday, 30 October 1959 finds 'Black Five' 4-6-0 No 45257 of Crewe North depot bustling southwards with a fairly lengthy van train, 'bread-and-butter' work for these engines on this route.

Below: It was rewarding to be in the right place to view trains passing, particularly if it involved locomotives of the same class. Here 'Royal Scots' Nos 46150 *The Life Guardsman* of Crewe North, northbound, and No 46161 *Kings Own* of London Camden, southbound, meet at Bishton Lane on Sunday, 6 May 1956.

Below: No fewer than 22 of the 842 Stanier 'Black Five' 4-6-0s were fitted with Caprotti valve gear. They weren't universally popular, but the last pair of engines, incorporating all the later refinements and easily identifiable by the provision of ugly high running plates, seemed to enjoy enhanced status on West Coast main line duties. No 44687 of Longsight depot skims along southbound from Colwich on Saturday, 25 July 1959.

Shugborough Tunnel, 4½ miles south of Stafford, is an example of a tunnel that was superfluous from an engineering standpoint; it merely 'burrowed' under the beautifully manicured estate of nearby Shugborough Hall. This produced the twin advantages of preserving the estate in one piece, and banishing the railway from the gaze of the second Lord Lichfield and his successors. Officially, it is the last tunnel on the WCML before Eglinton Street, Glasgow, some 270 miles to the north. However, the 'overbridge' at Preston Brook, Cheshire, always seems to me to qualify as a tunnel!

Top: Recovering from a signal check at Rugeley TV, red 'Duchess' 4-6-2 No 46244 *King George VI* of Carlisle Upperby depot strides purposely forward with a 16-coach northbound train. The normal BR standard coach formation has been strengthened by four extra LMS vehicles on this summer Saturday, 9 July 1960.

Middle: As late as 1960, lengthy goods trains on the West Coast main line could still be in the charge of LNWR Class 7F 0-8-0s — 'Super Ds' — or even Midland Class 4F and 3F 0-6-0s. Here, 0-8-0 No 49002 of Nuneaton depot wheels a lengthy northbound freight at Bishton Lane on Saturday, 9 July 1960. The Stanier revolution, let alone the diesel revolution, had yet to seriously affect the motive power used on this traffic!

Below: A southbound express, in the charge of 'Royal Scot' 4-6-0 No 46127 *Old Contemptibles,* leaves Shugborough tunnel on a Sunday afternoon in the autumn of 1957.

The Staffordshire village of Norton Bridge was (and indeed is) a busy place for watching trains, again between two facing junctions, one situated there and the other at Stafford, five miles to the south.

Top: 'Royal Scot' 4-6-0s were common currency at Norton Bridge at all times. Here, No 46138 *The London Irish Rifleman* of Holyhead depot approaches from the south on Sunday, 30 April 1961. Points of interest include the distinctive 'Scot' driving posture, and the late survival of the pre-July 1956 BR 'cycling lion' emblem on a main line locomotive tender. Preparations for the impending electrification are apparent above the ballast.

Middle: A chance 'overtake' is captured at the road bridge at Shallowford, Norton Bridge, on Sunday, 7 May 1961; nicely clean red Stanier Pacific No 46240 *City of Coventry*, a London Camden-based engine, has little difficulty overtaking Fowler '4F' 0-6-0 No 44548 of Stoke on an Up freight. Both of these locomotives were built at Crewe, in 1940 and 1928 respectively, a mere 12 years apart.

Bottom: Demotion for *Duke of Sutherland* — unrebuilt 'Patriot' 4-6-0 No 45541 of Nuneaton depot has been reduced in status to powering the train containing the boring machine for overhead electrification mast foundation laying. This duty, on Sunday, 5 March 1961, required a movement of some 80yd every 10min!

Top: 'Jubilee' 45556 *Nova Scotia* of Crewe North depot, in nicely clean condition, is leading an equally smart LNER Thompson corridor coach at the head of a Down train at Norton Bridge on 30 April 1961.

Below: Although Crewe North depot looked after the spectacular steam power of the WCML, it was the other Crewe LMS depot, South, that was responsible for 'bread-and-butter' power. These were the locomotives that worked parcels, freight and mineral traffic away from Crewe in seven different directions, as well as being first call for passenger substitutions. The 40 Stanier Class 5 2-6-0s were, of course, numerically less common than the 4-6-0s and 2-8-0s, but most were allocated to Crewe or depots within a 50 mile radius of Crewe. Thus the sight of No 42950 of Crewe South heading south with a long freight on Monday, 2 November 1959 was a familiar one at Norton Bridge.

Left: The turnout of the engines – and indeed headboards – of the flagship West Coast route trains was often not of the best, in part due to the complexity of locomotive rostering on such a busy route, and the shortage of labour for such mundane work by this time. Green Stanier Pacific No 46237 *City of Bristol* of Carlisle Upperby depot makes steady progress after a signal check. It is passing Izaak Walton's cottage at Shallowford with the northbound 'Royal Scot' on Sunday, 18 October, 1961. The crew are both visible in the picture but unfortunately not clearly against the light!

Crewe was a legendary place in the world of railways and perhaps the most well-known railway town amongst the general public. As well as being an interchange point for seven major radiating routes, it was also home to by far the largest locomotive works in the country, which in its heyday was extending its activities to making much else in the field of railway engineering.

Crewe, originally Church Coppenhall, was a hamlet in the rural countryside of the Cheshire gap until 1837, when it was discovered by the forerunners of the London & North Western Railway, Significantly, it was equidistant from the early engineering strongholds of the Black Country and Lancashire areas. In the scenes on these pages, the great era of steam traction was soon to end, and the gradual decline of Crewe as a railway town was under way.

Top: The first of two views of the Stephenson Locomotive Society's 'Three Summits' railtour of Sunday, 5 July 1964, which commemorated the approaching demise of the last remaining Stanier Pacifics. The outward leg, from Crewe to Carlisle over Shap, was in the hands of red No 46251 *City of Nottingham*, a known strong performer. Here at Platform 2 at Crewe, a mere 200yd from home base at Crewe North, it is about to set out.

Middle: The third stage of the journey from Leeds City to Crewe was over Standedge summit, and 'Jubilee' No 45647 *Sturdee* of Farnley Junction, Leeds, made a memorable contribution to the day; it is here seen at the end of its stint at Crewe's Platform 5. The other stages, from Carlisle to Leeds employed green No 46255 *City of Hereford*, and from Crewe to Birmingham New Street utilised No 46155 *The Lancer*. What a superb day out!

Below: In June 1964, Ivatt Class 2 2-6-2 tank No 41229 of Crewe North depot busies itself on empty carriage shunting duties at the north end of Crewe station, Platform 7 bay. This push-and-pull fitted locomotive was employed on Crewe to Northwich local passenger workings until their cessation early in 1960, but continued to run regularly over that route on parcels traffic, in addition to pilot duties at Crewe, as seen here.

Although the 50 Stanier Pacifics were also based at depots in London, Liverpool, Carlisle and Glasgow, it was Crewe North depot, with its specific expertise and proximity to the locomotive works, that had special responsibilities for keeping these exceptionally large and powerful (and indeed expensive!) locomotives earning their keep. Here are two views at their 'lair'.

Top left: Crewe North's half-roundhouse was a Pacific stronghold. Green No 46227 *Duchess of Devonshire* of Glasgow Polmadie keeps company with home-based red No 46251 *City of Nottingham* on Sunday, 8 October 1961. No 46227 was in its last year of service, one of the first to be withdrawn in late 1962. No 46251 was in the last batch to be withdrawn in late 1964.

Top right: A famous engine indeed is seen in Crewe North yard, also on Sunday, 8 October 1961; it is the pioneer LMS 'Royal Scot' 4-6-0, No 46100 of the same name. This was a Derby-allocated engine at the time, probably at Crewe for repair attention. In the background, the overhead catenary is strung up above the Holyhead line as far as the then-new electric depot.

Below: BR Standard Class 2 2-6-0 No 78017 of Stoke shed is here working a short freight alongside Crewe station in July 1964. The engine shows evidence of a 'quicky' repair at Crewe Works that did not extend to a total repaint – common practice in the last years of steam. No 78017's early years were spent struggling over Stainmore summit in the Pennines whilst allocated to Kirkby Stephen depot.

Crewe Works was the largest locomotive works in Britain and arguably the most efficient, with a large yard surrounded by separate workshops to cater for every locomotive, indeed engineering need. These views show something of the diversity visible to the observer on a visit.

Above: On Sunday, 7 August 1960, LNWR 'Super D' '7F' 0-8-0 No 49437 of Edge Hill, Liverpool, BR Standard '9F' 2-10-0 No 92150 of Saltley, Birmingham, and LMS Stanier '8F' 2-8-0 No 48248 of Crewe South were very much part of BR's front-line freight fleet. They were receiving the 'full treatment' in the Paint Shop. Within a few years, major repair work to freight locomotives would not include such careful cosmetic treatment. (The 'Super D' was here obscured by another engine, making a 'line up' picture impossible.)

Above left: This scene seems more reminiscent of Horwich than Crewe! These three Lancashire & Yorkshire Railway veterans were employed as Crewe works internal shunters on Wednesday, 5 April 1959. They were three of nearly a dozen engines of LYR origin employed at Crewe in the late 1950s/very early 1960s. The tank engines, Nos 51412 and 51444, were members of the Barton Wright/Aspinall rebuilt '23' class. No 52441 was an Aspinall-designed '27' class tender engine. Note the new BR Type 2 diesel on the left – it is No D5032 for those interested, later to become well known on the North Yorkshire Moors Railway.

Left: A close up of No 52441 in 1960, when works engine cleaning seems to have ceased.

Chester was an important railway centre, overshadowed a little by Crewe, 21 miles to the east, but nevertheless busy and attractive to enthusiasts who favoured a greater Great Western presence, and even some minor LNER activity at Chester's other station, Northgate. Finally, London Midland power reigned supreme.

Left: There are plenty of spectators on Chester's main platform as work-stained Stanier '8F' 2-8-0 No 48423 of Birkenhead depot gently drifts through with a Class H freight consisting of oil tanks for a Wirral refinery.

Below: Chester Midland depot, coded 6A, was an important district headquarters, but was past its best days by Friday, 24 August 1962, when 'Royal Scot' No 46114 *Coldstream Guardsman* of Holyhead, home-based 'Black Five' No 44916 and Fairburn Class 4 2-6-4 tank No 42270 were present.

Left: 'Britannia' Pacific No 70052 *Firth of Tay* of Crewe North depot calls at Chester General for water on Tuesday, 28 July 1964. A former Glasgow Polmadie engine, No 70052 was one of the last to retain handrails on the deflectors, which were mostly removed after the 1955 serious derailment at Milton near Didcot involving No 70026 *Polar Star*, when it was likely that the handrails had obscured the driver's vision.

Hooton, on the busy GWR/LMS joint line from Chester to Birkenhead, was a good place to watch trains, with a generous track layout and wide platforms making station photography easy.

Left: Stanier 'Jubilee' 4-6-0 No 45563 *Australia,* a long-time Manchester Patricroft engine that is here nearing the end of a final two-year stint at Warrington Dallam, calls at Hooton with a day excursion from Birkenhead Woodside to Llandudno and Betws-y-Coed. The date is Monday, 7 June 1965.

Below: Early on the morning of Saturday, 10 December 1966, several photographers were in the right place to record the last 'Crab' 2-6-0 in service, No 42942 of Birkenhead, leaving Hooton for Stanlow oil refinery as BR Standard '9F' No 92069 approached the junction, heading for the Birkenhead area. A group of us had cleaned No 42942 in a very cold Birkenhead shed during the previous night.

Right: In the middle of the day on 10 December 1966, Stanier Class 4 2-6-4 tank No 42548 bursts from a bridge south of Hooton station into the frosty countryside with a Birkenhead Woodside to London Paddington train. Unsurprisingly, this filthy Birkenhead-based engine is in its last couple of months of service, and makes a huge contrast with the smart condition of the leading BR Mk 1 brake coach, newly repainted in blue-and-grey livery.

Birkenhead, on the west side of the mile-wide mouth of the River Mersey, a ferry-ride away from Liverpool, was where the railway activities of those great rivals, the GWR and the LMS, came together, and not forgetting some LNER involvement. Freight transhipment was carried out on both shared and separate dockside wharves, all under the 'gaze' of huge cranes.

Left: Birkenhead Woodside station was a joint LMS/GWR establishment. It was a cold, somewhat foreboding place, contained within high walls and a grimy overall roof. There were sharp curves at the end of every platform leading immediately into a dank tunnel. But it had 'atmosphere'! Here Stanier 2-6-4 tank No 42482 of Chester Midland is just on the move with an express for London Paddington, which will reverse at Chester and gain 4-6-0 power. A few years earlier, this would have been a Chester West turn with a GWR 2-6-2 tank. The date is Saturday, 10 April 1965.

Below: A comparison of the Hughes Horwich-designed 'Crab' 2-6-0 on the right, and the Stanier Crewe-built development of it on the left, at Birkenhead depot on Sunday, 3 June 1962. No 42885 has just been transferred from Nuneaton to Birkenhead but still wears a 2B shedplate, whilst No 42981 is transferring in the other direction. Will the shedplates be swapped? For the record, No 42885 had been involved in the disastrous Penmaenmawr 'Irish Mail' collision of 1950 with 'Scot' No 46119.

The North Wales coast main line from Chester to Holyhead of 1848 was used by a comprehensive selection of LMS and BR locomotives in the days of steam. Its close proximity to the coastline for many miles might not have been to the liking of all holidaymakers, but the railway enthusiasts and photographers amongst them had few complaints! Steam operation ceased along here gradually during 1966.

Top: The fine setting at Colwyn Bay, with the promenade, pier and Little Orme to the right, and the Great Orme at Llandudno to the left. Centre stage belongs to 'Jubilee' 4-6-0 No 45647 *Sturdee* of Leeds Farnley Junction depot, heading for home with the summer 12.30 Llandudno to Leeds City train on Monday, 22 August 1966.

Middle: On Tuesday, 6 September 1960, the 'Emerald Isle Express', 7.30am Holyhead to London Euston, was in the capable hands of Stanier 'Princess Royal' Pacific power. Here, on time at 8.48am, now preserved No 46203 *Princess Margaret Rose* of Liverpool Edge Hill depot is seen approaching Colwyn Bay station. Note the spacious railway site, with the Down slow line far away to the left. No 46203 shows evidence of repaired front-end damage, including locally repainted cylinder cover, new bufferbeam rivets, and – most unusually – circular instead of oval buffers.

Right: On Monday, 22 August 1966, a pick-up goods eases along the slow line avoiding Colwyn Bay passenger station behind Stanier Class 8F 2-8-0 No 48458, a long-term Mold Junction engine relocated to Chester Midland for the last year of its existence, following Mold Junction's closure.

As already indicated, the North Wales coast route hosted a wide variety of locomotive types, a further selection of which are shown here. Steam had an undisputed grip on this area in 1959 and 1960.

Top left: At Llandudno Junction, the fireman of ex-works 'Royal Scot' 4-6-0 No 46131 *The Royal Warwickshire Regiment* is waiting to transfer the guard's 'tip' to the driver for the onward journey to Holyhead on Sunday, 16 May 1959. No 46131 was at this time a Longsight-based locomotive.

Top right: A walk to the western end of Llandudno Junction station was usually rewarded with steam activity. Here, Holyhead 'Black Five' No 45056 awaits departure for home, and locally-based Ivatt 2-6-2 tank No 41235 busies itself on carriage shunting, on Monday, 18 May 1959.

Left: On Wednesday, 7 September 1960, a likely motive power shortage saw a very begrimed Sutton Oak, St Helens, BR Standard Class 4 2-6-0 No 76078 accelerating a lengthy evening 'Class A' passenger train out of Colwyn Bay, photographed from the footbridge steps outside Rhos College for Girls. The driver made a thrashing hand gesture as he passed by, attempting to coax the maximum effort out of his overloaded engine.

More activity at this important double-junction . . .

Top: The driver of locally based Ivatt Class 2 2-6-2 tank No 41235 awaits the road to move empty stock to the carriage sidings on Monday, 18 May 1959. This engine was one of the earliest of this useful type to be withdrawn from service, at the end of 1962.

Middle: There is no mistaking the ex-works condition of red 'Duchess' Pacific No 46236 *City of Bradford* of Carlisle Upperby depot, about to leave Llandudno Junction for Holyhead on Saturday, 10 September 1960. The 105-mile run from Crewe to Holyhead provided an excellent virtually water-level route for 'bedding in' ex-works engines.

Bottom: The sojourn of BR Standard Class 4 2-6-4 tanks on the North Wales coast was quite short. No 80088 is heading for its home shed of Bangor, light engine, on Saturday, 16 May 1959. Within six months, this engine was transferred to the Brighton area of the Southern, only returning to Wales for destruction at Swansea in 1965.

The North Wales coast main line provides some interesting sights for the observant traveller, none more so than Conway. Here, a convenient park and bowling green gave a grandstand view!

Above: The Conway tubular bridge of 1848 was designed to harmonise with adjacent Conway castle, to the left of it in these views. Stanier Class 5 4-6-0 No 45180 is heading home to Holyhead with an afternoon train on Saturday, 16 May 1959.

Below: Although the Llandudno branch saw LNER-design engines of Classes B1 and K3, the Holyhead main line normally did not, and certainly nothing in the Pacific category! Here, on Sunday, 21 August 1966, Peppercorn 'A2' 4-6-2 No 60532 *Blue Peter*, by this time the sole survivor of the class based at Aberdeen Ferryhill depot, heads a featherweight six-coach enthusiasts' railtour from Manchester to Holyhead on this rather dismal day at Conway.

Right: During engineering rebuilding work at Manchester Piccadilly station, formerly London Road until 1958, the LNWR goods station alongside it, Mayfield, was used for passenger trains. Here, unrebuilt 'Patriot' 4-6-0 No 45520 *Llandudno* of Longsight depot takes hold of its train, the 3.05pm to Cardiff on Tuesday, 9 June 1960. On the right, parcels duties are being undertaken by Class 8F 2-8-0 No 48465, also of Longsight depot, later to be a Buxton survivor.

Below: An April 1964 scene at Manchester Longsight depot, featuring 'Black Five' No 44748, the last Caprotti 4-6-0 of nine to survive at the depot, and No 42845, a Gorton-based 'Crab' 2-6-0 whose driving wheelset was in course of repair in the nearby machine shop. Longsight depot, opened in 1840, had less than a year to remain a steam depot. Today it is a 'Pendolino' servicing facility, though remarkably with much of the old infrastructure still in place.

The London & North Western Railway route from Manchester to Leeds crosses the high Pennine ridge by means of the three-mile-long Standedge tunnels between Diggle and Marsden. The link, completed in 1849, eventually comprised four tracks in two single bores and one double bore. In the steam era, water troughs for locomotive replenishment were provided on the tracks at the western end of all of the tunnels.

Left: On Saturday, 4 December 1965, a double-headed 'Jubilee'-hauled railtour was routed from Stalybridge to Diggle via the now closed Micklehurst loop, which effectively formed a pair of slow lines on the opposite side of the valley from the main line, usually negotiated by freight traffic. Here No 45654 *Hood* of Newton Heath depot leads No 45596 *Bahamas* of Stockport as they 'roar' towards the short Butterhouse Tunnel, just before joining the main line at Diggle Junction.

Below: The bleak prospect at Diggle Junction is evident in this view of a WD 'Austerity' 2-8-0 that is just starting to drift downhill towards Stalybridge and the Manchester area with a train of Yorkshire coal, on Saturday, 4 December 1965. The Pennine ridge that is visible in the background is pierced by the Standedge tunnels. The 1 in 125 gradient at this point is highlighted by the true horizontal alignment of the signalbox.

Left: Although strictly within the North Eastern Region from mid-1956 onwards, this view of the eastern (Yorkshire) end of the Standedge tunnels shows the harsh environment in this rugged part of the Pennines. A dirty but capable 'Black Five' 4-6-0 has just completed the westbound climb of 10miles from Spen Valley Junction, and enters one of the two single-bore tunnels, 3miles 62yd long under the 1,300ft high massif of Standedge Moor. Note the solidly-built works of the diverted water course on the right. Such long single-bore tunnels, two each both here and at Woodhead, were the least pleasant aspects of Pennine steam footplate work – 'hell holes' might be the appropriate term to use!

Above: For many years, small but robust 0-6-0 tender engines of the Lancashire & Yorkshire Railway would struggle out of Manchester northwards and eastwards towards the Pennines through the district of Newton Heath. What greeted me on Thursday 9 June 1960 was the exact opposite of this! The peace of Newton Heath station was hardly interrupted by the passage of recently ex-Crewe Works '9F' No 92017, newly allocated to the vast motive power depot in the background, principally for Ancoats to Rowsley freights through the Peak District. This, however, is a featherweight civil engineers' train heading out of Manchester for the Castleton depot.

Below left: Slattocks – a name not easily forgotten! The Lancashire & Yorkshire main line to Leeds via Summit Tunnel climbs northwards out of urban Manchester into this rural area of animal grazing land before reaching Castleton triangle and Rochdale. '8F' 2-8-0 No 48057 of Northwich depot makes a fine sight, with a memorable smoke and steam effect, on the cold morning of Saturday, 16 December 1967.

Below right: The Whitworth branch from Rochdale was a quiet branch line, originally part of the through line to Bacup, and rarely saw any spectacular railway activity. An exception occurred on Sunday, 19 February 1967, when just before closure, preserved Keighley & Worth Valley Railway-based LYR Class 21 '0F' 0-4-0 saddle tank No 51218 worked three return brake van trips over the line. Members of several local railway societies 'take the air' (cold) near Shawclough on one of the trips.

Top: The Lancashire & Yorkshire Railway main line from Manchester to Leeds pierced the formidable barrier of the Pennines beneath Shore Moor by means of the 1½-mile long Summit (or Littleborough) Tunnel, completed in 1840. For many years, one of the most interesting trains to traverse this route was the lengthy Newcastle (Heaton) to Manchester (Red Bank) empty parcels van train, which usually required double-headed steam power both north of Leeds with North Eastern locomotives, and west of Leeds with London Midland engines. Here, on Sunday, 3 July 1966, 'Britannia' No 70015 *Apollo* and 'Black Five' No 45200, both of Stockport Edgeley depot, double-head the train towards the short Winterbutlee Tunnel, just before Summit Tunnel, on the 1 in 182 gradient. A group of us had cleaned No 70015 with paraffin and (not enough) oil, but the condition of No 45200 completely defied us, in the early morning at Farnley Junction shed, Leeds.

Middle: Another route which breasted the Pennine barrier was the one which linked North Lancashire with the Manchester to Leeds LYR route at Stansfield Hall, a triangular junction east of Todmorden. Its summit, in the open countryside at Copy Pit, was synonymous at the end of the steam era with Stanier and 'Austerity' 2-8-0s working flat out on freight trains, both front and rear. There were also unaided holiday-season passenger trains from east of the Pennines to Blackpool, usually with 'Jubilee' or 'Black Five' haulage. Here, we see 'Jubilee' No 45739 *Ulster* of Wakefield depot leaving Holme Tunnel, near to the summit of the southbound climb to Copy Pit from Burnley, with a returning holiday train from Blackpool to the Yorkshire West Riding on Saturday, 23 July 1966.

Bottom: For once, the presence of gushing live steam to enhance the picture is not required; the sunny backdrop of Stansfield Moor, part of the Pennine range, creates a memorable spectacle. The last remaining 'Britannia', No 70013 *Oliver Cromwell*, is fresh out of Crewe Works and in fine fettle, exhibiting perfect combustion whilst working very hard. The train is a Roch Valley Railway Society tour of the last bastions of steam in Lancashire on Sunday 21 July 1968. The locomotive is seen here approaching Copy Pit summit after the northbound climb from Stansfield Hall, near Todmorden.

Undoubtedly the railway crossroads of the northwest, this important location brought together the industrious activities of the London & North Western and Lancashire & Yorkshire Railways, two major companies which were – surprisingly – amalgamated one year before the formation of the London, Midland & Scottish Railway in 1923. Their individual dominance of areas elsewhere had been necessarily channelled into joint operations in the Fylde Coast area to the northwest of Preston in the quest to benefit from the burgeoning development of Britain's premier holiday resort, Blackpool. Traffic was also busy through the area to its restrained southerly neighbour, Southport.

Top: Photographed from a departing Blackpool-bound train, red-liveried 'Duchess' Pacific No 46248 *City of Leeds* of Crewe North depot stands in Platform 5 at Preston with the 11.05am Birmingham to Glasgow train on Saturday, 28 July 1963.

Middle: Caprotti valve gear-fitted 'Black Five' 4-6-0 No 44745 of Southport depot makes a spirited departure from Preston's Platform 6 with train 1J63, the Manchester Victoria portion of the 11.25am from Glasgow Central on Monday, 22 June 1964. The engine is only a couple of months away from withdrawal from service.

Below: BR Standard Class 2 2-6-0 No 78041, locally based at Lostock Hall depot, busies itself on 22 June 1964 with carriage shunting duties in Platform 3, with the substantial trainshed of Preston providing the backdrop. Such duties were the preserve of 'Jinty' Class 3F 0-6-0 tanks until a short time previously.

This village, in the Fylde Coast area of Lancashire, became the location for the split of the two routes from Preston to Blackpool: to Central via Lytham and the coast, and to North via Poulton-le-Fylde. (A few miles north of Kirkham, a later alternative route to Central via Marton Moss diverged from the route to Blackpool North, but this is now closed.)

Top: In pouring rain, 'Jubilee' No 45694 *Bellerophon* of Wakefield depot is heading a day trip special train from the West Riding to Blackpool via Copy Pit on Whit Sunday, 6 June 1965; the day was not a particularly good choice for sunshine at the seaside!

Middle: Whit Monday, 30 May 1966 sees 'Britannia' No 70010 *Owen Glendower* of Carlisle Kingmoor depot bringing a special from Heald Green, Cheshire, to Blackpool through Kirkham.

Bottom: Most of the 'west coast' resorts saw 'east coast' locomotives on special trains at holiday periods; Blackpool received LNER Thompson 'B1' 4-6-0s and Gresley 'K3' 2-6-0s. Here, 'B1' No 61276 of York depot passes Kirkham with a special from the North Eastern Region via Copy Pit on Whit Sunday, 6 June 1965.

Blackpool was one of a select few British holiday resorts that boasted very busy steam locomotive depots. (Bournemouth and Brighton were others.) The establishments near Central and North stations were geared to servicing holiday excursion locomotives on short turn-rounds, in addition to the heavy ordinary passenger traffic that radiated through Lancashire.

Of the two principal Blackpool stations, the earliest, Blackpool North (Talbot Road when opened in 1846) had the friendliest feel about it and unsurprisingly was the most photogenic, with interesting curvature and less of Central's 'regimentation'. It was also a 5min walk from my work lodgings, which were conveniently next door to the home of a locomotive driver in the summer of '64!

Top: On Monday, 29 June 1964, the 17.10 to Manchester Victoria was powered by 'Jubilee' No 45675 *Hardy* of Leeds Holbeck. This loco was just ex-Crewe Works, in unlined livery but at least painted green, as befits an express passenger engine in the twilight of a distinguished career, much of it at Leeds.

Middle: At Blackpool Central depot on Sunday, 28 June 1964, Stanier 'Jubilee' 4-6-0s Nos 45562 *Alberta* of Leeds Farnley Junction and 45661 *Vernon* of Manchester Newton Heath sit out the afternoon awaiting the call to head homewards.

Below: Staple power for many duties at Blackpool was appropriately the Stanier 'Black Five' 4-6-0, with both residents and daily visitors. Here, on the same day as above, No 45241 of Stoke and No 45033 of Crewe South are prepared over the soundly constructed heavy-duty ash disposal pits for the journey home.

Blackpool South station was a superb place to watch and photograph trains, particularly those accelerating onto the direct line to Preston via Marton Moss which closed in 1967. Photographically, a calm sunny wind-less evening was preferable at this relatively bleak spot.

Above left: 'Jubilee' 4-6-0 No 45562 *Alberta,* a survivor until 1967, heads a return excursion to the Leeds area on Sunday, 28 June 1964; smoke by arrangement!

Above right: One of the four 'Black Fives' equipped with a self-weighing tender, No 44697 of Newton Heath depot, heads a Manchester train under the normal exhaust created by perfect combustion, on 28 June 1964. Steam survived at Blackpool in an increasingly limited way until the end of BR steam in August 1968.

Below: To the north of Blackpool, Fleetwood depot possessed a clutch of the rare (only 30) BR Standard Class 2 2-6-2 tanks for working local passenger trains in the Fylde Coast area. No 84018 spent all but six months of its 12-year existence on this work. Here it has just worked the 4.50pm from Preston to Blackpool Central via St Annes on Sunday, 28 July 1963, giving a lively run between stations.

All of the 55 'Britannia' Pacifics spent their last few years working some of the fastest and heaviest trains on the 141-mile section of main line from Crewe to Carlisle, and associated routes. Here are two scenes showing them running at high speed. The extinction of main-line steam in Britain was just weeks away.

Above: The 1 in 88 gradient for one mile southbound out of Lancaster Castle station was an impediment to stopping trains, but this was no problem at all for 'Britannia', No 70013 *Oliver Cromwell*. The locomotive is charging the gradient with a nonstop 'Farewell to Steam' special train organised by BR Scottish Region on Saturday, 1 June 1968. The location is near the former Lancaster Old Junction. No 70013 was the only active 'Britannia' survivor into 1968, and the only one ever to be based at Carnforth depot.

Below: In the more familiar latter-day scruffy external condition of London Midland Region-based 'Britannias', No 70016 *Ariel* of Carlisle Kingmoor tears through Hest Bank, between Lancaster and Carnforth, with a summer relief train on Saturday, 1 July 1967. The train is approaching the only seaside stretch, barely a mile long, that justifies the title 'West Coast main line' being applied to the 401 miles from London to Glasgow!

Carnforth in North Lancashire was an important railway centre from the earliest days of railways – 1846 in fact – and was ultimately to become one of the last operating centres for steam locomotives in Britain. Hence it was the focus for much enthusiasm and photography, which continued into the steam preservation era.

Above: A special train from Leeds 'corkscrews' its way into the Barrow line platforms at Carnforth on Saturday, 30 April 1966, in the charge of Leeds Holbeck-based 'Jubilee' 4-6-0 No 45593 *Kolhapur*. Here the locomotive will retire to the locomotive depot for servicing and turning, thereafter heading over Shap summit to Carlisle with this special.

Below left: LMS Class 3F 'Jinty' 0-6-0 tank No 47375 stands outside the shed, and is nearly at the end of a long career, spent mostly at Chester, on Sunday, 18 March 1962.

Below right: The LNWR 'Super D' 0-8-0s had a wide sphere of operation, indeed over most of the LNWR system. No 49449 of Carnforth, no stranger to climbing to Shap summit with heavy freight trains in earlier times, had recently finished its many years of service on 17 March 1963, and would soon be despatched to Horwich Works for cutting up.

The railway route around the Cumbrian Coast from Carnforth to Barrow and continuing to Whitehaven and Workington is one of the most spectacular – but unsung – in the country, typified by distant views of the Lake District fells on the right and quiet beachcomber sea shores on the left.

Below: The Kent viaduct of 1857, over the estuary of that name between Arnside and Grange-over-Sands, is the first of several low height viaducts on the route, giving wonderful broad vistas. Here, the only unnamed 'Britannia', No 70047 of Carlisle Kingmoor depot, heads the 13.20 Barrow to London Euston express on Friday, 9 July 1966, forming a totally BR Standard train.

Bottom left: Ulverston, on the Barrow line, is a distinctive station, situated on a steep gradient, and gave passengers on Down trains an opportunity to detrain onto platforms on either side of the line, making it necessary for all drivers and firemen to keep a good look-out. 'Black Five' No 44948 of Carnforth is seen working a heavy freight, banked (out of sight) by Stanier Class 4 2-6-4 tank No 42610 on Tuesday, 24 August 1965.

Bottom right: On the rainy day of 24 August 1965, the motive power for my return journey on the branch line from Ulverston to Windermere Lakeside was Ivatt Class 2 2-6-0 No 46441 of Carnforth, destined for preservation two years later. This is the run-round operation at Lakeside prior to the 14.00 departure. The Lakeside branch opened for business in 1869, and closed in 1965. The section from Haverthwaite to Lakeside reopened under preservation auspices in 1973.

Here are two more Cumbrian Coast line views in the Barrow area. Although steam traction survived here until quite late on, the relative inaccessibility of the area to enthusiasts and the dieselisation of most passenger services reduced the photographic opportunities compared with railways in other areas.

Above: At Pennington, six miles from Barrow, the summit of the Carnforth line is reached in each direction by steep gradients. Here, an eastbound train of empty 16-ton mineral wagons – a more typical '8F' 2-8-0 load – is headed by 'Black Five' No 45390 of Carnforth depot and is seen approaching the summit of the four-mile 1 in 76 climb in a businesslike fashion. The appearance of the locomotive has benefited from the attentions of an amateur cleaning gang during shunting operations in Kendal goods yard the previous afternoon. The date is Thursday, 1 August 1968, just two days before the end of normal steam traction on BR.

Left: A lucky photographic chance on the coastal section at Millom, 16 miles north of Barrow (9 miles 'as the crow flies'), on Saturday, 2 April 1966. On the right, Ivatt Class 2 2-6-0 No 46458 is the lead engine of a Carlisle Upperby pair (the other being No 46426), heading the Stephenson Locomotive Society 'Lakes and Fells' Railtour that has earlier traversed the Penrith-Keswick-Workington line. Heading towards us is ex-works BR Standard Class 9F 2-10-0 No 92233 of Carlisle Kingmoor depot, and the train consists of covered hopper wagons (Covhops) bound for Corkickle, further up the Cumbrian coast.

The Lancaster & Carlisle Railway line through Oxenholme, Westmorland, opened for business in 1846. Although the immediate locality has remained rural, the importance of the railway station from the outset as the junction for the expanding Lake District communities of Kendal and Windermere has ensured its survival on the railway map. It also proved to be a convenient location for the attachment of banking locomotives for the climb to Grayrigg and pilot locomotives for both Grayrigg and Shap inclines in steam days.

Right: Stanier Class 5 4-6-0 No 44816 of Lostock Hall, Preston, calls at Oxenholme on Sunday, 12 July 1964 with a southbound train. The overall roof of the Windermere branch platform is visible to the left. The branch opened throughout in 1847.

Left: Looking from the sloping field in the vee of the Carlisle and Windermere lines north of Oxenholme, Wakefield WD 'Austerity' 2-8-0 No 90707 clanks back up the gradient on the Windermere branch from Kendal with the return working of the morning pick-up freight on Saturday, 13 November 1965. The engine has a 'balanced wheels' circle on the cabside, although it is doubtful if 'Duchess' riding qualities were on offer from this much-travelled engine, far away from home and its regular haunts, such as Knottingley power station.

Right: This view of 'Britannia' No 70043 *Lord Kitchener* of Crewe North depot at Windermere terminus about to work the 11.10 to Crewe hides a tale. No 70043 had sticking drain-cocks on the driver's side, resulting in a continuous and annoying loud steam hiss. The driver had consequently acquired a serious headache which was cured by a) me dashing downhill to a chemist shop in Windermere town for Aspirins, b) two of us helping the fireman to turn No 70043 on the Windermere hand-operated table whilst the driver watched from a nearby garden-type bench. All of this activity was in the course of a return footplate ride along the branch on Saturday, 15 May 1965. No 70043 was to last only a further three months in service, the second 'Britannia' to be withdrawn.

Above: Here is the result of a cleaning session in Kendal goods yard! On Thursday, 1 August 1968, Stanier Class 5 4-6-0 No 44894 of Carnforth climbs the 1 in 80 gradient from Kendal to Oxenholme with the afternoon Carnforth freight. It was a warm sunny day, and the cleaning activity, with ladders provided, was hot work for six of us. The finishing touch was a 24A Accrington shed plate commemorating a home of 'Black Fives', although not this one, up to seven years earlier.

Below: This was an unexpected sight at Staveley, Westmorland, on Friday, 8 July 1966. Stanier Class 5 2-6-0 No 42954, one of the last four of these locomotives based at Wigan Springs Branch, heads the 15.15 from Windermere to Liverpool Exchange. By this time, the quartet were mostly employed on local parcels and freight work in the Wigan area, so No 42954's 'afternoon out' in the Lakes was a most unexpected and welcome change.

Just north of Oxenholme, the West Coast main line immediately addresses the seven-mile climb to Grayrigg | summit, as shown by these scenes of Saturday, 13 November 1965, with steam at maximum effort.

Above: A lengthy fitted freight, unassisted at the rear, is here in the charge of 'Britannia' No 70003 *John Bunyan* of Carlisle Kingmoor depot. The steam sanders are working well, and the wisp of steam from the safety valves suggests that the internal condition of the locomotive is far better than its grimy external appearance suggests.

Below: At the same location, but viewed from the other side of the line, another Carlisle Kingmoor-based locomotive, 'Black Five' No 44902, gets into its stride with a lengthy freight, in this instance banked by Fairburn Class 4 2-6-4 tank No 42110 of Tebay depot for the climb to Grayrigg, after which the tank engine would leave the 'Black Five' to continue on its own.

The lower reaches of the climb to Grayrigg summit are accompanied by splendid views to the west over the Lake District mountain range. Higher up, the line penetrates the high fells, and enters the Lune Gorge at Low Gill. North of Tebay, a superb panorama unfolds on the climb to Shap summit.

Above: 'Black Five' No 45212 of Carlisle Kingmoor depot heads a lengthy mixed freight approaching the A684 Northallerton to Kendal road bridge on the flanks of Hay Fell, about one mile north of Oxenholme. In the distance is Whitbarrow Hill, near Arnside. The date is Saturday, 12 August 1967. No 45212 escaped the cutter's torch to find a home on the Keighley & Worth Valley Railway and later the North Yorkshire Moors Railway.

Left: At Castle Green on the outskirts of Kendal, 'Jubilee' 4-6-0 No 45593 *Kolhapur* (named after an Indian province) makes light work of the Grayrigg climb with a Leeds to Carlisle enthusiasts' special train on Saturday, 30 April 1966. The train had reversed at Carnforth in order to tackle the Shap route, rather than the more usual route from Leeds to Carlisle over Ais Gill. The engine had obviously been very thoroughly cleaned at Leeds Holbeck, its home depot.

Just after Grayrigg summit to the foot of Shap incline at Tebay, rail passengers are treated to the delights of the Lune Gorge, a dramatically narrow but fairly level valley, which allows trains some fast running amidst glorious mountain scenery.

Above: Evidence of the level nature of the Lune Gorge section is provided by the presence of Dillicar water troughs, one mile south of Tebay. 'Black Five' 4-6-0 No 45227 of Lostock Hall depot, Preston, takes on a goodly tender-full of water from a full trough on the evening of Saturday, 5 August 1967. The train is the 11.55 London Euston to Carlisle, a summer Saturday extra booked for steam haulage north of Preston. The view shown here is no longer available, having now been obliterated by the M6 motorway.

Below: If locomotives required assistance over both Grayrigg and Shap inclines, it was usual to attach the assisting locomotive in front of the train engine. Thus, Fairburn Class 4 2-6-4 tank No 42210 of Tebay depot is piloting a 'Black Five' No 45109 of Warrington Dallam with a northbound parcels train on Saturday, 16 July 1966. The location is Greenholme cutting, 1½ miles north of Tebay and well into the four mile 1 in 75 climb to Shap summit. No 42210 was a Scottish Region Ardrossan-based locomotive until the reorganisation that followed the Clydeside electrification took effect.

The 40-mile-long line from Penrith to Workington via Keswick, through the spectacular scenery of the Lake District, would have been a prime candidate for retention today as a tourist line. However, the desire of the road protagonists to widen the A66 trunk road alongside the narrow south shore of Bassenthwaite Lake, utilising the railway trackbed, was always likely to cause a major confrontation at some stage.

Top: A last steam special on Saturday, 2 April 1966 was attended by superb weather, bright sunshine following an overnight snowfall. Here, a brace of Ivatt Class 2 2-6-0s, always a photogenic combination, and quite typical of activity on the line, pause at Keswick station, a rather grand edifice for the traffic on offer. Both 2-6-0s, Nos 46458 and 46426 had been cleaned at their home depot of Carlisle Upperby by interested enthusiasts and railwaymen; they were complemented by a tidy set of LMS coaches, worked up from Manchester Victoria by none other than LNER Class A3 4-6-2 *Flying Scotsman*.

Middle: Between Penrith and Keswick, the line twists and turns with the mountains of the Lake District as a backdrop. This is a view between Troutbeck and Threlkeld from the front coach of the special train amidst the sunshine and snow.

Below: After the arrival at Workington, there was an opportunity for both engines to take water before tackling the journey to Barrow by way of the inland Moor Row route: steep, circuitous and prone to mining subsidence. The Metrovick Co-Bo diesel on the left only outlasted steam by a couple of months – certainly these 20 machines proved to be poor replacements for the products of Stanier and Ivatt!

On this double page, activity on the climb to Shap summit is shown, with the tremendous brute force of steam power evident at the front and rear of trains ascending the classic four-mile long 1 in 75 gradient. The place was made famous by probably the best known of British railway photographers, Eric Treacy.

Right: A special train of prefabricated track panels for the advancing West Coast main line modernisation and electrification is 'urged' out of Tebay by '8F' 2-8-0s Nos 48426 of Buxton and 48517 of Saltley. Both locomotives are working flat out at the start of the severe climb to Shap summit, 915ft above sea level, on Saturday, 30 April 1966.

Below: Working equally hard at the back of the train is Fairburn Class 4 2-6-4 tank No 42225 of Tebay. The engine has just buffered up to the train a minute or so earlier, and the combined sound of the three locomotives is set to echo around the hills for the next few minutes. All this is a far cry from No 42225's previous service on Marylebone-Chilterns trains when based at London's Neasden depot. This photographic location, on the slopes of Loups Fell, is now completely obliterated by the M6 motorway earthworks.

Above: A scene of wonderment for this young lad at Scout Green, about halfway up the Shap climb, on Saturday, 7 October 1967. (He'll be in his early 40s now.) Stanier Class 5 4-6-0 No 45444 of Lostock Hall depot, Preston, attacks the climb with a mixed freight, including seven of the soon-to-be-discarded cattle wagons.

Below: At the rear is BR Standard Class 4 4-6-0 No 75037 of Tebay, originally used on London Euston commuter trains when based at Bletchley depot, but now thrust into the more rugged activity of Shap banking work following the demise of the Fairburn 2-6-4 tanks. The reign of these BR Standard locomotives on Shap banking duties lasted just less than one year.

Penrith was at one time the location for the junction off the West Coast main line to the CKP – the Cockermouth, Keswick & Penrith Railway, and also the North Eastern Railway route to Kirkby Stephen and over the Pennines at Stainmore summit to Darlington. Today, it no longer has junction status, but remains an important railhead for a large area of Cumbria.

Here, some activity is shown at the well-known photogenic location just south of the station on Saturday, 17th July 1965.

Right: BR Standard '9F' 2-10-0 No 92114 disturbs the peace of Penrith with a southbound freight. The engine was new to Westhouses, near Chesterfield, in 1956 and was only fully available for 'mountain service' a month before this picture was taken on 17 July 1965, when transferred to Carlisle Kingmoor depot. In fact, the overdue allocation of these engines to Carlisle revolutionised freight working in the Borders area right at the end of the steam era. Penrith No.1 signalbox is in the background.

Above: Passenger services on the Keswick line involved diesel multiple-unit trains, apart from the Workington portion of the 'Lakes Express' to and from London Euston; there was also the daily steam-hauled pick-up goods train. On 17 July 1965, a pair of clean Ivatt Class 2 2-6-0s, Nos 46458 and 46455, head off the Keswick line into Penrith with another more sporadic steam incursion, the annual specials to and from the Keswick Convention, a noted religious festival.

Right: The Keswick Convention special continued to London Euston after reversal with 'Britannia' No 70031 *Byron*, newly reallocated from Crewe North to Carlisle Upperby, both depots relevant to this journey. The fireman has built up a good head of steam for the southbound climb to Shap summit, 13 miles distant, little trouble for this competent machine.

Here, we continue northwards to reach the immediate environs of Penrith station, opened by the Lancaster & Carlisle Railway in 1846. The 'Penrith for Ullswater' station nameboards reminded all through travellers of the town's proximity to Lakeland.

Above: Very few steam passenger services survived in the Penrith area through until the mid-1960s, but here is one. Fairburn Class 4 2-6-4 tank No 42154 of Carnforth depot heads south at 10.26am with the Workington/Keswick portion of the 'Lakes Express', which will be added to the Windermere portion at Oxenholme for onward conveyance to London Euston. Note the cylinder drain-cock 'display', on Saturday, 17 July 1965.

Middle: A view of the south end of Penrith station, featuring 'Black Five' No 45216 of Rose Grove depot, Burnley, calling with a southbound train, probably the 10.35 Glasgow Central-Blackpool Central, on Saturday, 17 July 1965. Steam working over this section of the West Coast main line, from Carnforth to Carlisle over Shap summit, ceased on 31 December 1967.

Left: Just recently ex-Crewe Works – note the fresh paintwork and the clean white lagging of the boiler feedwater pipe – the one time *John Bunyan* – 'Britannia' No 70003 of Carlisle Kingmoor – leaves Penrith with the late-running 00.10 London Euston-Glasgow Central sleeping car train on Saturday, 2 April 1966. Passengers in the train, composed of a mix of BR and LMS vehicles, were sitting on top of their bunks resembling day passengers, as indeed they were at 09.30! The train was running some 3hr late on this snowy morning.

Having travelled from London to Penrith along the London & North Western Railway system, we now return to London to journey north once again, but this time on the tracks of the equally comprehensive Midland Railway system, ultimately reaching the gateway to Scotland common to both systems, Carlisle.

London St Pancras station comprises a huge single-arched trainshed roof 245ft wide and 100ft high, at the 'business end' of a handsome and distinctive Gothic style building housing a hotel and railway offices fronting onto Euston Road. The trainshed was designed by W.H. Barlow, and the building by Sir Gilbert Scott, and both were completed in 1868. It was every inch a main line station, but has been under-used for most of its existence, sharing many of its long-distance destinations with those of other London termini – Marylebone, Euston, King's Cross and Fenchurch Street. And its exit from London was through somewhat less populous suburbia than some other routes.

In 2007, St Pancras became 'gateway to Europe'.

Right: Under the huge trainshed roof, it is a fairly quiet time. 'Jubilee' No 45641 *Sandwich* of Nottingham shed is backing out of Platform 3, following the empty stock of the train that it has just brought in. This is the 'Robin Hood', 8.15am from Nottingham with a 10.30am arrival time in St Pancras. The date is Thursday, 2 April 1959.

Below: 'Jubilees', together with 'Black Five' 4-6-0s, formed the usual main line power seen at St Pancras for many years, but this is the scene on Platform 5 at the start of a valedictory trip on Saturday, 6 June 1964. No 45721 *Impregnable* of Crewe North depot was specially procured for the Locomotive Club of Great Britain 'North Countryman' railtour for Leeds, the first stage of a marvellous day out to Carlisle and an eventual return to King's Cross behind an 'A3' 4-6-2. Steam finished in general service in this area at the end of 1964, with the closure of Cricklewood depot. *Michael York*

Above left: Gothic architecture seemed popular on Midland Railway territory, and the main line passenger shed at Kentish Town, London, was provided with a distinctive backdrop for locomotive photographs more than one hundred years ago. Indeed, this view is nearly 50 years old! Stanier 'Black Five' No 44963, a well-liked Birmingham Saltley-based member of the 842-strong class, stands in the yard. It is no doubt engaged in a regular duty, powering the overnight train conveying freight traffic in box vans between the goods depots at Birmingham Landor Street and London Somers Town, just alongside St Pancras station, and usually routed via Wigston curve at Leicester. The date is Tuesday, 5 January 1960.

Above right: For many years, regular power for the London St Pancras suburban service was provided by the Fowler Class 3 2-6-2 tanks, a total of 70 of which were built, and of which no fewer than 22 examples were found in this area. On Sunday, 29 April 1962, No 40053 here (and 40020) were stored after the diesel invasion at Bedford, presumably in the best condition for future service. Many locomen would argue that there was no 'best condition' for these hapless engines, which elsewhere were 'shunted' around, unloved, from depot to depot in 'pass the parcel' manner. Their principal fault was a serious one for steam engines – they wouldn't usually steam very well!

Below: Another troubled beast was the Franco-Crosti version of the BR Class 9F 2-10-0, 10 of which were built and allocated to Wellingborough, Northamptonshire. In their original form, they were nothing short of a disaster, and were stored at Wellingborough for some months, if not years, until 'de-Crostified' at Crewe. Devoid of their pre-heater drum for steam supply, they were then actually demoted to '8F' power status, although not officially. Here, the then recently rebuilt pioneer Crosti No 92020 runs past Bedford motive power depot (MPD) on Sunday, 3 March 1963.

Here is the Midland side of New Street; its trainshed roof was found to be repairable after the bomb damage of World War 2, unlike the roof of the North Western side, which was damaged beyond repair, and had to be demolished. Trains started using these platforms in 1854, and steam in the area was gradually replaced by diesel traction between 1961 and 1966. Regular long-distance passenger trains were the first to succumb to diesel locomotive haulage, followed by regular local passenger trains to diesel railcar operation, leaving a few extras, seasonal reliefs and parcels traffic to diminishing steam haulage.

Above: The classic main line motive power at New Street was the 'Jubilee' class of 4-6-0, at both sides of the station. This 1955 view at Platform 9 features No 45660 *Rooke*, one of nine members of the class well maintained at Barrow Road, the former LMS shed in Bristol, for working express trains to York and Leeds, these journeys always involving a long trek northwards. *Lyn Whitworth*

Right: There is plenty of steam from the cylinder drain-cocks here at Platform 10 of New Street, as two 4-6-0s, 'Black Five' No 45268 of Saltley double-heads 'Jubilee' 4-6-0 No 45648 *Wemyss* with a Bristol express. They are about to do battle with the curving 1 in 75/80 climb to Five Ways station through four tunnels – Holliday Street, Canal Street, Granville Street and Bath Row. The date is Saturday, 6 June 1959.

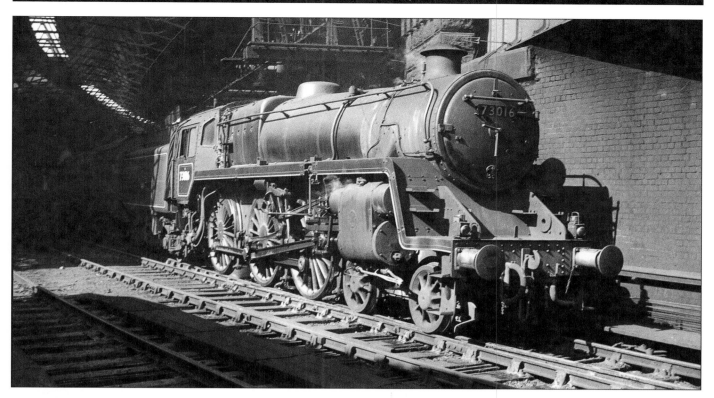

Above: Strong sunlight highlights the features of BR Standard Class 5 4-6-0 No 73016 of Sheffield Millhouses depot at the south end of Platform 7 on Saturday, 28 March 1959. These engines were never squadron-performers on the Derby-Bristol route, but at various times Sheffield, Derby, Gloucester and Bristol had small batches to supplement the regular diet of Stanier Class 6P 'Jubilee', and Class 5 4-6-0s. The BR 'Standard 5s' were liked or tolerated, depending upon who you asked, but No 73016 looks very purposeful in this view.

Middle: On Saturday, 29 August 1964, the 09.10 Weston-super-Mare to Sheffield Midland relief passenger train waits to leave Platform 8 at New Street with Canklow, Rotherham, 'B1' 4-6-0 No 61327, which was working through from Bristol to Sheffield. These engines were, in many cases, past their best, and needed some 'coaxing' on their seasonal long-distance forays. Ahead can be seen the 'B1's' tortuous exit through the 254yd-long New Street South Tunnel to the next stop at Derby.

Bottom: It was common practice at busy times to position a Stanier 'Black Five' on the centre road of the Midland side of New Street facing south to double-head or replace an ailing main line locomotive. On this occasion, the engine was of above average interest, being one of the four named examples of the type, No 45156 *Ayrshire Yeomanry* of Liverpool Edge Hill depot.

Duddeston Road was a busy (if slightly illegal!) place to watch trains on the Midland Railway eastern exit from Birmingham. This was, and is, a very busy part of the rail network, with main routes diverging to Leicester and Derby at Water Orton, 7½ miles away, and to Walsall via Sutton Park at Castle Bromwich, 5½ miles away. Here at Duddeston Road, the Birmingham avoiding line (the 'Camp Hill line') leaves the passenger route to New Street in central Birmingham. In steam days, all classes of traffic were seen, and much of the motive power required was supplied by Saltley depot, the access to which was also controlled by Duddeston Road signalbox.

Above: Fowler Class 4 2-6-4 tank No 42417 bustles towards Birmingham with a local passenger train as Stanier Class 5 4-6-0 No 44981 heads eastwards with freight. Both are Saltley locomotives, and passing by their home base.

Middle: A heavy southbound freight gets under way from Duddeston Road in the capable hands of Saltley's BR Standard '9F' 2-10-0 No 92164. Speed is being built up for the 1 in 85 climb to Camp Hill on the Birmingham avoiding line.

Below: Banking this train from Saltley to Camp Hill is BR Standard Class 4 2-6-0 No 76036, newly allocated to Saltley from the London area, and making this a truly 'standard' freight train.

Saltley Motive Power Depot in east Birmingham was the principal former Midland Railway engine facility in the area, and home to 150 steam locomotives in the mid-1950s. Established in 1868, it succumbed to total diesel traction in March 1967. Final closure as a diesel stabling point, a mere shadow of its former self, came in 2007.

Top: Almost the extremes in freight power, Class 3F 0-6-0 No 43668 of 1900 is prepared for duty alongside Class 9F 2-10-0 No 92151, new to Saltley in 1957. It is hard to believe that early in the 20th century, Saltley men on such '3Fs' worked regularly to Upper Bank, Swansea, via Hereford and Brecon and lodged there! The date of the picture is Tuesday, 8 November 1960.

Middle: A good choice for a 'where is it?' competition. We are actually 'out at the back' of Saltley's No 1 roundhouse, and 70E Salisbury-based 'Merchant Navy' 4-6-2 No 35007 *Aberdeen Commonwealth* is being prepared for a Warwickshire Railway Society trip from Birmingham New Street to Doncaster and York on Sunday, 11 October 1964.

Below: Saltley in the evening – this is a small group of engines in No 3 roundhouse on Thursday, 20 October 1966. The ex-Crosti 2-10-0 No 92029 was allocated to Saltley at the end of its career and was universally declared a very poor machine. Consequently, it spent an inordinate amount of time in the roundhouse, and is here 'surrounded' by the much more highly rated 'Black Five' No 44872, and the consecutively numbered but conventional '9F' No 92030 of Banbury.

The eastern exit from Birmingham was busy with traffic all through the week, and the possession of a lineside permit was useful, if not essential, to record the activity, usually well away from any public access points.

Right: Midland Class 2P 4-4-0 No 40407 of Derby bustles along through Washwood Heath sidings with an afternoon Derby to Birmingham local in the mid-1950s. In the background is Bromford Bridge, a strategic point on Birmingham's outer ring road and in those days adjacent to the Birmingham racecourse. Racegoers arrived by rail at flimsy wooden platforms alongside the slow lines. *Lyn Whitworth*

Right: At the country end of Birmingham racecourse was Castle Bromwich station. 'Jubilee' No 45585 *Hyderabad* of Derby has been 'bumped off' expresses by 'Peak' diesels, and reallocated to Burton. It is entering the 'golden mile' of the slow line with a coal train. This line was subject to permissive block signalling arrangements, allowing slow freights to queue up, nose-to-tail, awaiting yard entry, and causing engine crews to rack up plenty of overtime pay doing 'not much'!

Right: Here is another 'old soldier' operating after its best days. 'Patriot' 4-6-0 No 45541 *Duke of Sutherland*, now allocated to Nuneaton depot, wheels a freight from Nuneaton to Birmingham onto the slow line at the east end of Castle Bromwich station on Saturday, 17 September 1960.

Top: This is the long straight from Castle Bromwich to Water Orton, and it is here being negotiated by LNER Gresley 'V2' 2-6-2 No 60919 of Dundee Tay Bridge depot, heading the evening Bromford-Tees steel train on Tuesday, 12 July 1966. The 'V2' was returning to Scotland following an unsuccessful visit to the Southern Region for the LCGB 'Green Arrow' railtour. (It was failed at Nine Elms in favour of 'West Country' No 34002.)

Middle: The first of two views from the grandstand of Water Orton West signalbox. LNWR 'Super D' 0-8-0 No 49361 has just arrived from Bescot via Sutton Park and reversal at Washwood Heath, and will soon be ready to return to Wolverhampton directly via Sutton Park with a trip freight on Saturday, 30 May 1964. Water Orton was an important point for interchange of traffic between the Midland Railway network and the Black Country.

Bottom: The extremely wet night and morning of Saturday, 6 June 1964 finds ex-Crosti No 92026 of Kirkby-in-Ashfield depot heading towards Birmingham with a lengthy coal train – in not the most pleasant of footplate conditions. Only two of the ex-Crostis were ever stationed at Kirkby, and then only for a very short period.

The so-called 'Sutton Park branch' of the Midland Railway was always a backwater in steam days, although a strategically useful freight route that avoided central Birmingham, with a sparse local passenger service. It linked a triangular junction near Water Orton on the Birmingham to Derby and Leicester lines with Walsall on the LNWR network and Wolverhampton with connections to the LNWR and GWR. In more recent times, line closures and changed traffic flows have resulted in the Sutton Park line becoming an important link to Bescot freight yard near Walsall.

Right: Fowler Class 4F 0-6-0 No 44160 of Saltley depot saunters downhill through Sutton Park station with an oil tank train for Bromford Bridge on a pleasant day in the summer of 1960.

Below: The woodland peace of Sutton Park nature reserve is disturbed by the thunder of green but grimy 'Duchess' Pacific No 46235 *City of Birmingham*, on the morning of Sunday, 5 April 1964. The train is the featherweight Kilburn (London) to Carlisle parcels train, diverted from the Trent Valley line by engineering work and from the normal Birmingham diversionary route by electrification: hence Nuneaton-Water Orton-Walsall-Portobello-Bushbury-Stafford was the only route available. This train was rostered for Class 40 haulage, but shortages caused this engine and No 46256 to have appeared a fortnight earlier. 'Duchesses' weren't officially route-cleared for this line, but who was looking?

The Boy Scouts World Jubilee Jamboree at Sutton Park from 29 July to 14 August 1957 brought an intensive period of special trains to Sutton Park, Streetly and Sutton Coldfield stations, the like of which had rarely, if ever, been seen before. To give some idea, there were in the order of 400 special passenger trains, bringing locomotives borrowed from all over the London Midland Region. No fewer than 103 *different* 'Black Fives' appeared!

Left: Streetly station on 1 August 1957 saw a special freight with Class 4F 0-6-0 No 44559, proudly displaying its 71G Bath shedplate, and with single line Whitaker tablet catcher seemingly at the ready! This engine was originally Somerset & Dorset Joint Railway No 59 of 1922.

Right: Star of the show was specially named 'Britannia' No 70045 *Lord Rowallan* of Holyhead depot, here seen about to leave Streetly at 5.40pm on 1 August 1957 with VIP guests for the return journey to London St Pancras. Lord Rowallan was the Chief Scout at the time.

Left: A van special passes Streetly with the pioneer Caprotti Standard Class 5 No 73125 of 84G Shrewsbury depot, then just one year old. To break up the long sections through both Streetly and Penns stations, temporary signalboxes and block signalling equipment were specially installed for the Scout event at both places.(Streetly's is seen in the lower left of the picture of *Lord Rowallan*.)

This is the busy junction of the Derby and Leicester lines, 7½ miles east of Birmingham. The footbridge, linking the village centre with 'The Dog' public house and the small housing estate beyond, has always been a favourite place for train watching, particularly on warm summer evenings!

Above: The 9.30am Yarmouth Vauxhall to Kings Norton approaches Water Orton on 4 August 1962 with Fowler Class 4F 0-6-0 No 43940 of Saltley in charge. The engine exhibits Saltley's trademark 'black Jap' smokebox sealant paint, which gives a false impression of overall engine cleanliness, fooling many caption writers. Note the replacement signalbox programme in progress in the background.

Right: On 4 August 1962, the 10.10am Newcastle to Cardiff summer Saturdays-only train approaches Water Orton behind Thompson 'B1' 4-6-0 No 61033 *Dibateg* of Sheffield Darnall depot. This was a particularly prolific period for 'B1s' working into Birmingham from the north-east, to the delight of local linesiders, and on this occasion No 61033 worked through to Gloucester Central.

The Birmingham to Derby main line was completed in 1839, and connected two important railway centres across the Midlands of England; it was always extremely busy with both passenger and freight traffic, and being virtually a 'water level route' for most of the way, traffic would 'get a move on'.

Above: The peace at Tamworth High Level is disturbed by the arrival of a Newcastle to Bristol train with 'Jubilee' 4-6-0 No 45690 *Leander* at 'the business end' on Saturday, 15 June 1963. Only a few minutes earlier, I had arrived at Tamworth clutching my cheap day return ticket from Birmingham New Street behind Bristol Barrow Road shedmate No 45682 *Trafalgar*. 'Those were the days', indeed!

Below: Burton-on-Trent locomotive depot opened in 1870 and closed to steam in 1966. It seemed to be a well-run establishment of standard Midland Railway design, with a complement of local passenger and freight locomotives. It was a little different to most depots in that it operated some 0-4-0 tanks and small 0-6-0 tanks, all employed on the myriad of brewery railways in the town. Express passenger work in the area was usually handled by Derby shed, a mere 11 miles to the north. A skilled fitting staff were given the job of looking after the five 'Crab' 2-6-0s with poppet valve gear. Later, after the diesel revolution, no fewer than 20 three-cylinder 'Jubilee' 4-6-0s were deposited in their care. But here is a 'regular', Stanier Class 8F No 48704, outside the depot on Monday, 20 February 1961.

KINGSBURY

This important location on the Birmingham to Derby line, 11½ miles from the second city, became a junction for the Baddesley branch in 1878. A further junction was added in 1909, when the Midland Railway constructed a direct line to Water Orton, avoiding Whitacre and Coleshill, and this was used by all expresses and most through trains thenceforward.

Above: Viewed from the slope of the Up platform at the now long-closed station, Fowler Class 4F No 44539 of Coalville depot 'jangles' northwards with a lengthy merchandise freight on the evening of Saturday, 9 April 1960. It is often forgotten that these modestly-sized engines hauled prodigious freight trains over lengthy distances until their final few years in service.

Below: BR Standard '9F' 2-10-0 No 92074 of Saltley depot heads towards Birmingham with mineral empties on Wednesday, 30 March 1966. Note the roof of Kingsbury Station Junction signalbox behind the train. No 92074 was originally an Eastern Region engine, one of 30 allocated to 38E Annesley depot for the 'windcutter' freights to Woodford Halse. As such, it is fitted with the LNER-looking BR1F tender with high water capacity, rather than the LMS-looking BR1C tender with high coal capacity that was fitted to local '9Fs'.

The emphasis here is again on heavy freight on the Birmingham to Derby main line, but we move a little further north, on the section between Tamworth and Burton-on-Trent. This route continues to be a crucial and busy part of the rail network today.

Above: WD 'Austerity' 2-8-0 No 90456 of Frodingham depot had only a few months left in service when photographed approaching Haselour (sometimes known as Wigginton) water troughs with a northbound steel train on Saturday, 16 October 1965. The bridge in the background carries the A453 main road from Tamworth to Ashby-de-la-Zouch. This is a fast main line, and the ride qualities of this high mileage Frodingham 'Austerity' might well be imagined!

Below: Completing the freight quartet is Toton's '8F' No 48185, approaching Wichnor Junction with a coal train for the Birmingham area on Tuesday, 25 August 1959. The home signals in the background control the junction for the LNWR route to Lichfield Trent Valley High Level and the Midland main line to Tamworth High Level, as well as the Down loop (it is Up to Derby). Wichnor Junction signalbox is situated directly behind the camera.

The East Midlands county of Leicestershire saw some of Britain's earliest railways. An extensive network of independent lines developed through the nineteenth century, all eventually being absorbed into the empires of the Midland, Great Central, Great Northern and London and North Western companies. Nowadays, relatively few of these lines survive, and indeed some closed before the Beeching axe of the early 1960s. Two extreme examples of locomotives that survived into the last days of steam in the north west of the county are shown below.

Right: Good day! Midland Railway Class 2F 0-6-0 No 58148 looks out of its Coalville home depot on Sunday, 21 April 1963. This 1876-built engine was one of several of the type kept at Coalville, always at least two at any given time, for working the Leicester West Bridge daily goods train through the tight clearance bore of the 1832-built Glenfield Tunnel. In 1964, for this line's last two years of existence, two BR Standard Class 2 2-6-0s, with specially cut-down cabs, were drafted in as replacements, eventually being Leicester-based after the closure of Coalville depot. With the withdrawal of three Brighton 'Terrier' tanks imminent, No 58148 was soon to become the oldest locomotive on British Railways.

Below: Mineral empties pass through Castle Donington, on the Stenson Junction to Sheet Stores Junction freight line on Saturday, 16 October 1965, behind BR Standard '9F' No 92129 of Banbury depot. This route formed an important link from the West Midlands to the huge marshalling yard at Toton, Nottingham, and it remains an important freight line to this day.

England's smallest county contained some undulating and pretty countryside crossed by long-distance rail routes of both LNWR and Midland Railway ancestory.

The adjacent villages of Harringworth and Seaton provided above-average railway interest, set as they are in rolling countryside, with magnificent open vistas.

Left: Without doubt, the most spectacular engineering structure was Harringworth Viaduct on the erstwhile Midland main line from London St Pancras to Nottingham via Kettering, Oakham and Melton Mowbray; the route is now normally used only by freight traffic. The 82-arch viaduct is three-quarters of a mile long, and 60ft above the wide valley of the River Welland. On Saturday, 8 May 1965, a Stanier '8F' 2-8-0 makes the crossing with a northbound freight train, viewed from the pretty stone-built village of Harringworth.

Below: One of the last passenger 'push-and-pull' services in the country linked the two cross-country routes west of Peterborough; these were the LNWR line from Rugby to Peterborough at Seaton, and the Midland route from Leicester to Peterborough at Stamford. The 9¾ mile Seaton to Stamford service consisted of six return trips daily in the charge of Ivatt or BR Standard Class 2 2-6-2 tanks from Market Harborough, sub-shedded at Seaton. Here is No 84006 at Seaton with the 12.38pm train on Saturday, 8 May 1965. In 1966, Seaton ceased to exist on the railway map, when both the main line and the branch were closed.

DERBY

Derby was (and is) one of the most important places on Britain's railway network. Railways came to Derby in 1839, and within a few years it was a route centre, with railways radiating in seven directions. It was the headquarters of the Midland Railway, the second largest of the constituent LMS companies, and site of some of the largest locomotive and carriage building and repair workshops in the country. The locomotive depot on the adjacent site closed to steam early in 1967, new steam locomotive building at the works having ceased in 1957, and steam repairs in 1964. The works continued to play a major part in diesel locomotive, multiple-unit and rolling stock repairs for many years, although even these activities have reduced dramatically in recent times.

Top left: Here is the standard view of the south end of Derby station on Tuesday, 1 July 1958. 'Royal Scot' No 46152 *The King's Dragoon Guardsman*, recently released from West Coast main line work and one of six allocated to London Kentish Town depot, is about to leave for London St Pancras. To the left, locally-based 'Black Five' No 44839 awaits further instructions.

Top right: Deeley Class 0F 0-4-0 tank No 41529, from Barrow Hill, has made its last journey to Derby for scrapping on Friday, 23 June 1961.

Right: Fowler Class 2F 0-6-0 dock tank No 47164, christened in chalk 'The Flying Flea', has obviously just recently been dealt with at the works. It enjoys a test run alongside the running shed on the dull morning of Monday, 20 February 1961, effectively during transfer from Speke Junction to Birkenhead depots.

Below: Derby repaired many types of locomotives, but particularly of Midland Railway design, as epitomised by Fowler '4F' 0-6-0 No 44249, ex-works and ready for delivery back to its home shed of Staveley Barrow Hill. Note the impressive line of repaired locomotives alongside the running shed roundhouses in the background.

Here are three views of Derby station on Saturday, 29 August 1964.

Left: LNER 'B1' 4-6-0 No 61327 of Canklow, Rotherham, at Platform 3, 'gassing up' for the continuous climbing ahead, culminating in the 1 in 100 gradient from Sheepbridge to Bradway Tunnel. The semaphore signals form a fine backdrop at the north end.

Below: Another view of 'B1' No 61327 with the 09.10 summer Saturdays-only Weston-super-Mare to Sheffield Midland train. The engine is working through from Bristol to Sheffield. Note the spotter 'encampment' on the far platform.

Left: The station pilot is BR Standard Class 2 2-6-0 No 78020, recently transferred from Nottingham to Derby for these duties. It is viewed from Platform 5.

This is just a brief visit to the territory of that fiercely independent and well-regarded pre-Grouping company, the North Staffordshire Railway, which was based at Stoke-on-Trent.

Above: On Tuesday, 24 April 1962, Stanier two-cylinder Class 4 2-6-4 tank No 42564 of Stoke stands outside the plain and simple three-road shed at Uttoxeter. Also present inside were Nos 42443 and 42609 of the same class; although Uttoxeter had its own small allocation, by this time most of the locomotives seemed to be 'floaters' between here and the parent shed, Stoke. The work at Uttoxeter had reduced considerably with the closures of the Churnet Valley and Buxton lines, and the shed closed to steam at the end of 1964.

Below: Alton Towers had already become an important inland resort whilst the Churnet Valley line was still in operation as part of the national network. Consequently, there were special trains from surrounding areas on most bank holiday and summer weekends, also during the main holiday weeks. On Tuesday, 4 August 1959, whilst waiting in a queue for the return train to Birmingham New Street behind 'Black Five' No 44776 of Saltley, I 'clicked' sister engine No 45300 of Crewe South with a return train to the Potteries towns. A five-mile extension of the rapidly developing Churnet Valley Railway could see sights like this being repeated; fingers crossed!

MILFORD TUNNEL

This tunnel, on the Midland Railway Derby to Sheffield main line six miles north of Derby, is 855yd long and effectively forms the topographical boundary between the gentle Midlands plain and the rugged Peak District.

A convenient road bridge over the line to the north of the tunnel's ornamental northern portal produced these views on Tuesday, 24 April 1962.

Above: Snowplough-fitted '8F' 2-8-0 No 48158 – the Hornby-Dublo one – of Leeds Holbeck depot heads north with a merchandise freight.

Left: Fowler Class 3F 0-6-0 No 43669 of Derby shed works a southbound pick-up freight homewards. As I wound the film out of my camera 10min later, LNER 'A2' 4-6-2 No 60516 *Hycilla* followed the '3F' to Derby with the 8.15am Newcastle-Cardiff express, as a result of an engine shortage at York. One of the ones that got away!

By the 1960s, this historic line across the top of the Peak District was becoming an interesting anachronism attracting considerable attention from enthusiasts. The line dated from 1830, with sections of adhesion working interspersed with cable power over the steepest inclines.

These views were all taken during 'normal working hours', and away from the well-attended special trains, when, incredibly, enthusiasts were conveyed in open wagons!

Above: At the eastern end of the line, High Peak Junction formed the connection with the Derby to Manchester main line, just south of Cromford Wharf, with canal transhipment facilities, sidings and a small engine shed for the regular shunting engine at the foot of the first cable incline. Part of Cromford Wharf is visible behind the large retaining wall on the left as '8F' No 48332 of Burton depot heads a southbound main line freight on Saturday, 29 January 1966.

Right: At the top of the first incline, at a location known as 'Sheep Pasture Top', adhesion working resumed for the 1¼ miles to Middleton Foot, at the base of the second cable incline, high above the town of Wirksworth. The first of the 10 Kitson-built Class 0F saddle tanks, No 47000, is seen after work at lunchtime on Saturday, 29 January 1966. During a footplate ride a little earlier, the crew told me of a local miscreant who changed a set of points and caused this engine to run away and derail upside down at Steeplehouse in 1955. Who says vandalism is new?

Top: There was another locomotive shed at the top of Middleton incline, adjoining the cable winding house. It housed one or two ex-Ministry of Supply/LNER 'J94' class 0-6-0 saddle tanks for operation over the next adhesion section, the nine miles to Friden. This section included the steepest adhesion-worked incline on British Railways, the half mile at Hopton, which steepened to 1 in 14 near the summit. It is here being 'rushed' by 'J94' No 68006 on Wednesday, 2 March 1966, the warm dull day conveying little impression of the effort involved in lifting these two Midland Railway tenders conveying . . . water!

Middle: On the same section of line, at Longcliffe on Saturday, 9 May 1959, former North London Railway 0-6-0 tank No 58850 saunters along eastbound from Friden to Middleton Top. These engines preceded the 'J94s', lasting nearly 30 years in the role. This one, the last example in use, finished in service a few months later, and has since been actively preserved on the Bluebell Railway in Sussex.

Below: The last section of the line, the 2¼ miles from Friden to Parsley Hay, on the Buxton to Ashbourne line, was less restricted weight- and curvature-wise, and Midland Class 3F 0-6-0s, superseded in 1962 by Ivatt Class 2 2-6-0s, worked through from Buxton to Friden. Here is 2-6-0 No 46484 of Buxton near Newhaven, Derbyshire, on Wednesday, 2 March 1966. A footplate ride, and drive, included the exceptional offer of 'select your own photographic spot and stop the engine at it'. The C&HP was a remote operation, far away from Euston HQ! The Cromford & High Peak line closed completely as a result of diminishing traffic early in 1967.

To a certain extent overshadowed by the huge railway complex, including a large freight locomotive depot, at Toton on the edge of the city, Nottingham nevertheless had its own locomotive depot near to Nottingham Midland station, with some interesting photographic possibilities. Nottingham shed closed to steam in 1965.

Top: The standard Midland Railway roundhouse building forms the backdrop to BR '9F' No 92120 emerging for duty on Sunday, 22 June 1961, probably making the short 'hop' to its home depot of Leicester.

Middle: At the coaling plant, home-based 'Jubilee' 4-6-0 No 45667 *Jellicoe* looks in fine fettle, ready for a departure from Nottingham Midland to London St Pancras on Sunday, 24 July 1960. Within a few months, the squadron-entry to service of 'Peak' diesels would see steam bumped off most Midland main line passenger services, and *Jellicoe* sidelined at Burton-on-Trent.

Bottom: A brighter future lay ahead for pioneer Stanier Class 8F 2-8-0 48000, also Nottingham-based at this time, and still with plenty of active freight service ahead of it until 1967. The date of this picture was Sunday, 15 April 1962.

Some locomotives of Midland Railway pedigree were still hard at work in the Chesterfield area, lasting until the end of the steam era in the mid-1960s. This enabled two important examples to be saved for posterity.

Above: An agreement between the Midland Railway Company and the colliery company *circa* 1871 ensured that the main line company and its successors would continue to provide motive power at Blackwell 'A Winning' colliery near South Normanton, Derbyshire, for 100 years. The result was that, after Westhouses depot closed to general steam operation in 1966, three steam locomotives continued to be based there for maintenance during the colliery work. They were LMS 'Jinty' Class 3F 0-6-0 tanks Nos 47289, 47383 and 47629. Later, LNER 'J94' 0-6-0 saddle tank No 68012 arrived, following the closure of the Cromford & High Peak line. Here, No 47629 performs at the colliery on Thursday, 17 August 1967. No 47383 was also in use on that day, a few weeks before it was sold to Manchester-area members of the Severn Valley Railway.

Middle: Before the end of ordinary operations at Westhouses, Fowler Class 4F 0-6-0 No 44598 shunts the BR sidings on Sunday, 19 February 1961.

Left: A motive power provision agreement also applied at the extensive Staveley Ironworks complex north of Chesterfield. In this case, a stud of ancient 0-6-0 tanks and diminutive 0-4-0 tanks was maintained at Staveley Barrow Hill shed to service the works. Here is Midland Railway Class 1F (former 'half cab') 0-6-0 tank No 41875 resting between duties on Sunday, 17 February 1963. Staveley Barrow Hill closed to steam late in 1965, having been included in the Eastern Region since early 1958. No 41708 of the class was preserved.

One of the least popular line closures of the Beeching era involved the main route through the heart of the Derbyshire Peak District between Matlock and Peak Forest Junction. It opened in 1863 and closed in 1968. The lost link caused the cessation of direct passenger services between London St Pancras and Manchester Central, and all journeys from the East and North Midlands to Manchester then involved changes at Sheffield. It was a beautiful railway, although very expensive to maintain.

Above: 'Jubilee' 4-6-0 No 45622 *Nyasaland* of London Kentish Town depot emerges from Headstone Tunnel and crosses the River Wye at Monsal Dale viaduct with the 'Palatine', 7.55am from London St Pancras to Manchester Central on Monday, 1 August 1960.

Right: A close-up of Headstone Tunnel's northern entrance with Ivatt Class 2 2-6-0 No 46440 of Derby emerging light engine on 1 August 1960.

Below: 'Britannia' No 70017 *Arrow*, then fairly recently reallocated from Cardiff Canton to Manchester Trafford Park, shuts off for the viaduct and tunnel at the head of the 10.25am from Manchester Central to London St Pancras on 1 August 1960, which that morning would have passed No 45622 in Millers Dale station.

Proceeding north along the picturesque main line through the Peak District, the important junction station of Millers Dale was reached. Here, a shuttle service of steam-worked push-and-pull trains, later diesel railcars, was operated to the important spa town of Buxton, 5½ miles away, and inconveniently just off the Manchester main line. Millers Dale was a busy railway place, with a well laid-out station in a fabulous setting. Even on a Saturday afternoon, in this case Saturday, 24 June 1961, the trains, both passenger and freight, continuously rolled by!

Above: A freight from Rowsley yard enters Millers Dale across one of the two massive viaducts spanning the River Wye behind Rowsley's newly-acquired BR '9F' 2-10-0 No 92008.

Middle: No 92008's progress was impeded by a northbound express, and closely following this was an afternoon Ancoats, Manchester, to Rowsley freight headed by 'Jubilee' 4-6-0 No 45679 *Armada* of Newton Heath depot, running at speed downhill from the summit at Peak Forest. However, No 45679's glory days on really fast top link work from Carlisle Kingmoor were now over.

Bottom: A few minutes after No 92008 had departed, what appeared next? Well, No 92009, of course! Also Rowsley-allocated, the driver seemed proud of having charge of such an impressive machine for the 1 in 90 climb to Peak Forest summit. Originally fitted with a small tender, No 92009 bequeathed this to No 92079, the Lickey banker, to facilitate coaling at the primitive facilities at Bromsgrove, and thus No 92009 received No 92079's large tender in exchange.

BUXTON DUTIES

The only BR steam locomotives to operate in a Midlands county in 1968 were based at Buxton, Derbyshire, where fires were finally dropped on Saturday, 2 March. In the few weeks before that, no fewer than four of the eight Buxton '8F' 2-8-0s had been cleaned by enthusiasts overnight, for workings to Gowhole (Manchester line) and Hindlow (Ashbourne line).

Smoke by arrangement! No 48775, on loan to Buxton from Patricroft, Manchester, rounds the, by then, only remaining side of the Buxton triangle at Peak Forest Junction and attacks the 1 in 90 climb to Peak Forest summit on Saturday, 10 February 1968 with a late morning trip to Gowhole yard. This engine was, numerically, one of the last three Class 8Fs, only added to BR stock in 1957, and carried the Middle East redesigned top feed clack valves with external shut-off cocks, the large protective casing for which is clearly visible in this view.

Left: Another engine loaned to Buxton at the end of steam was No 48191 of Heaton Mersey, seen here at the photogenic spot of Chinley South Junction on Saturday, 17 February 1968. It is working the 10.20am Gowhole to Buxton freight on the relentless climb at 1 in 90 to Peak Forest summit.

Below: A genuine Buxton-based Class 8F, No 48744, responded well to the cleaning treatment and I awarded it a personal bufferbeam repaint in red. It is here seen after overnight snow, approaching Chinley station on Saturday, 10 February 1968. A fitting end to Buxton steam and the cold nights of cleaning activity!

Chinley was an important triangular junction on the Midland Railway system in the Peak District, where the line to Sheffield (the Hope Valley line) left the Derby to Manchester line. All of these routes were busy with all classes of passenger and freight traffic, the latter through the 24hr day. Railways came to Chinley in 1866, and steam traction disappeared – from freight service – early in 1968.

Above: Just after the end of steam operations, a Manchester Rail Travel Society enthusiasts' special appeared at Chinley on Saturday, 20 April 1968, hauled by Stanier 'Black Fives' Nos 45110 of Bolton and 44949 of Newton Heath. These engines worked the train Stockport Edgeley-Buxton-Peak Forest-Romiley-Hyde-Stalybridge. It is safe to say that the British Transport Police had no office at Chinley! The background of this view is dominated by the mountain Kinder Scout, the highest point in the Peak District.

Right: Here is Chinley in normal times, with few passengers, it has to be said, boarding the 1.05pm all stations to Sheffield Midland with BR Standard Class 5 4-6-0 No 73155 of Canklow, Rotherham, on Wednesday, 22 August 1962. The last batch of these engines was largely unwanted by the Eastern and North Eastern Regions – as seen here – but by the end of the year, No 73155 was despatched to Eastleigh for 4½ years of meaningful work on the Southern Region main lines.

It could legitimately be said that the Midland Railway route across the Pennines from Chinley to Dore, on the outskirts of Sheffield, was one that really should not have been built, when the terrain to be traversed is considered. To make use of the east-west running valleys of the Rivers Hope and Derwent, it was necessary first to pierce Totley Moor, 1,300ft above sea level, by the 3½-mile long Totley Tunnel, the second longest on BR. Then there was Cowburn ridge, 1,700ft above sea level, crossed by the 2-mile long Cowburn Tunnel. It was an underground railway outside London, and opened throughout in 1893.

Left: One of the last steam workings over the line was the 07.00 Chinley to Sheffield stopping train, worked by Buxton engines and men. Ivatt Class 2 2-6-0 No 46485 hustles an appropriate set of LMS Stanier-era coaches away from Chinley on the approach to Cowburn Tunnel on Saturday, 2 July 1966.

Below: At the eastern end of the route, '8F' No 48208 of Heaton Mersey depot heads coal empties from Gowhole to the Sheffield area through Grindleford station on Thursday, 29 December 1960.

Left: Fairburn Class 4 2-6-4 tank No 42084 of Low Moor depot, near Bradford, emerges from the depths of Totley Tunnel with the 4.31pm Sheffield Midland to Chinley local on 29 December 1960. This Low Moor fill-in turn had brought Lancashire & Yorkshire Railway 2-4-2 tanks to Chinley a few years earlier.

In early British Railways days, the whole of the former Midland Railway from London St Pancras to Carlisle was within the London Midland Region. But in mid-1956, the Leeds area was included within the North Eastern Region, and in early 1958, the Sheffield area was included within the Eastern Region. The only difference that could be discerned by enthusiasts was the gradual increase in the use of ex-LNER locomotives in ex-London Midland territory, but it never became substantive. In this book, with a couple of convenient exceptions (Staveley and Bradford Forster Square), we leap from Totley Tunnel to Skipton to avoid the lost London Midland territory.

Above: In the yard of Skipton locomotive shed are two types long associated with the area. Fowler Class 3F 'Jinty' 0-6-0 tank No 47427, north end pilot and a long-term Skipton resident, is seen with Hughes 'Crab' Class 5 2-6-0 No 42834 of Carlisle Kingmoor depot, on Saturday, 18 August 1962. Skipton closed to steam in 1967.

Right: Into the final days of steam, 'Jubilee' 4-6-0 No 45593 *Kolhapur* stands in Skipton station with a railtour for Carnforth and Carlisle on Saturday, 30 April 1966, and draws admiring glances from two local lads, such was the cleaning effort in Leeds Holbeck roundhouse.

The Yorkshire Dales region can readily be described by the somewhat over-worked expression 'an area of outstanding natural beauty'. But the scene has been transformed in places, out of economic necessity. Such a result is shown in the upper view.

Above: The 8¾-mile long Grassington branch from Embsay Junction was completed by the Midland Railway in 1902, and closed to passengers in 1930. Freight traffic continued until 1969 and then the railway was cut back 1½ miles, still enabling it to continue to serve Rylstone Quarry, now owned by Tilcon. Steam working finished on Saturday, 1 June 1968, when BR Standard Class 4 No 75019 of Carnforth depot brought a ballast train out of the quarry, witnessed by a horde of photographers. A group of us spent the 'small hours' cleaning No 75019 on Rose Grove depot, Burnley, and I added the correct specification smokebox numberplate, fashioned out of hardboard with raised balsa wood numerals. The footplate crew and favourable weather did the rest!

Below: Ivatt Class 4 2-6-0 No 43113 of Lancaster Green Ayre depot eases out of Gargrave station on time at 2.04pm with the combined 12.05pm from Morecambe Promenade and 12.20pm from Carnforth to Leeds City train on the glorious day of Thursday, 17 August 1961. The backdrop features the broad valley of the Eshton Beck looking upstream towards Rylstone and Grassington.

This hamlet, in the Aire valley, was transformed into a railway community with the opening of the Midland Railway line from Skipton to Ingleton in 1849. Its importance increased when it became a junction following completion of the Lancashire & Yorkshire line to Burnley in 1880, but it was the total linkage of Leeds with Morecambe, Carnforth and Carlisle that increased Hellifield's importance, as evidenced by the provision of a locomotive depot, goods yard and carriage sidings.

Above: 'Black Five' No 45495 arrives with the Saturday 10.35am Carnforth to Leeds City train on 13 February 1965. To the right is Hellifield motive power depot, home to preserved locomotives by this date. Incidentally, No 45495 was the engine involved in the Lichfield Trent Valley disaster of 1946.

Middle: The RCTS 'Rebuilt Scot' railtour called at Hellifield on 13 February 1965 for an abortive water stop during the course of its circuitous journey from Crewe to Carlisle with Class 7P 'Royal Scot' 4-6-0 No 46115 *Scots Guardsman*. By this time, only five 'Scots' were in operation, and by the end of the year, No 46115 became the only survivor.

Bottom: A ballast train arrives on 13 February with Skipton-based Class 4F 0-6-0 No 44462, another engine in the autumn of its days. It has already been provided with overhead warning signs and cabside yellow diagonal warning stripes denoting 'banned south of Crewe' owing to the erection of overhead electrification apparatus, a major reduction in the operating range of such locomotives, brought about by their chimney height.

In steam days, freight traffic was prolific on the route from Settle Junction to Wennington Junction, and continuing on to either Lancaster/Morecambe/Heysham or Carnforth/Barrow. These two views were recorded near the summit of the 1½-miles of 1 in 100 gradient between Giggleswick and Eldroth, North Yorkshire, in 1967.

Above: The much-travelled 'Jubilee' No 45647 *Sturdee*, now Leeds Holbeck-based for its last few months, rounds the curve to the summit with a Leeds to Heysham mixed freight. A problem with our cleaning effort at Holbeck during the previous night was that the cab roof could not be reached successfully because of the shed roof smoke vents! This is Saturday, 15 April 1967.

Below: No special treatment was available for Class 5 No 45111 of Burnley, here battling hard – and steaming well – at the summit on 15 July 1967. During its last decade of service, this locomotive was based at Crewe South, Crewe North, Longsight, Monument Lane, Upperby, Willesden, Chester, Mold Jcn, Llandudno Jcn, Holyhead and finally Rose Grove!

Travelling further west from Settle Junction, the Midland Railway routes to Carnforth (joint with the Furness Railway) and Lancaster parted at Wennington Junction.

Today, Wennington is no longer a junction station, the line to Lancaster having closed in 1967.

Top: Fairburn Class 4 2-6-4 tank No 42154 of Carnforth depot has just brought the 12.20pm from Carnforth into Wennington and this formed one portion of the 12.30pm Morecambe Promenade to Leeds City train onwards from Wennington. The date is Saturday, 15 May 1965.

Middle: Push-and-pull fitted Ivatt Class 2 2-6-2 tank No 41215 stands ready for duty at Lancaster Green Ayre depot on Saturday, 18 August 1962. In the left background are the overhead stanchions of the then operational 6.6kV Lancaster-Morecambe-Heysham overhead line, and the handrails of the bridge taking that route across the River Lune, now a road bridge. Behind No 41215 is BR Standard Class 5 No 73171 of Leeds Holbeck depot.

Below: The view from Morecambe Promenade platform of recently ex-Crewe Works Stanier '8F' 2-8-0 No 48707, a former Central Wales and Somerset & Dorset engine recently divorced from its usual haunts by dieselisation and closure, and reallocated to Lostock Hall, Preston. It was shunting in the sidings on Saturday, 15 May 1965.

Above: A pleasant way to view the Settle & Carlisle line in summer was by travelling on the 3.40pm Bradford Forster Square to Carlisle stopping train. We have strayed here onto what became, from mid-1956 onwards, North Eastern Region territory. BR Standard Class 6 4-6-2 No 72008 *Clan Macleod* of Carlisle Kingmoor depot is about to leave Bradford for its 105-mile-long trans-Pennine journey on Saturday, 1 May 1965.

Right: A view of Ribblehead Viaduct from the 10.14 summer Saturdays-only train from Leeds City to Glasgow Central via Settle and Kilmarnock on Saturday, 5 June 1965. The competent motive power at the head is LNER Peppercorn-designed 'A1' Pacific No 60154 *Bon Accord*, a Leeds Neville Hill-based engine with normally little work to do by this time, and hired out to Leeds Holbeck for this 238-mile outing, usually unbalanced by any return train. The train itself originated at Birmingham New Street at 06.40, for Bradford Forster Square, but was officially diverted and extended to Glasgow on summer Saturdays. The following two summers saw ever-cleaner 'Jubilees' being used on this and the 14.11 from Leeds (09.25 from London St Pancras), the 'A1s' having gone to the breaker's yards.

Left: At Garsdale station, high in the Pennines, 'Britannia' Pacific No 70008 *Black Prince* of Carlisle Kingmoor depot arrives with the 16.37 Carlisle to Bradford Forster Square local, consisting of three LMS coaches; a 143-ton loco pulling a 90-ton train! The date is Saturday, 1 May 1965.

The Settle & Carlisle main line across the top of the Pennines, defined as the 73 miles between Settle Junction, North Yorkshire, and Petteril Bridge Junction, Carlisle, was completed following massive financial and constructional problems by the Midland Railway in 1875. The Midland wanted its own route to Scotland independent of its West Coast and East Coast rivals, so a railway was driven through extremely difficult terrain, involving many tunnels and viaducts. The result has fascinated railway enthusiasts ever since, particularly during the closure threat era of the 1970s and 1980s. Nowadays, it is a very busy railway once again. Steam activity finished on the route in ordinary service at the end of 1967, although the line has been a popular choice for hosting preserved steam-hauled trains since 1978.

Above: Throughout the summer of 1967, a group of enthusiasts kept two of the last three 'Jubilee' 4-6-0s – all based at Holbeck shed, Leeds – in very clean condition. They were rostered for working the two summer Saturdays-only trains from Leeds to Glasgow Central – the 10.17 and 14.11 from Leeds. Here, No 45562 *Alberta* heaves the 10.17 train past Stainforth rocks on the approach to the short Taitlands Tunnel on Saturday, 5 August 1967. The locomotive is three miles into the almost unbroken 15-mile climb from Settle Junction to Blea Moor.

Below: In the afternoon of 5 August 1967, the powerful pairing of '9F' 2-10-0s Nos 92125 of Carlisle Kingmoor and 92077 of Carnforth blast up the 1 in 100 climb to Blea Moor, seen here just above Horton-in-Ribblesdale. They are heading a heavy train of new concrete-sleepered track panels for use in the Carlisle area as a prelude to electrification, and have another six miles of hard collar ahead. The *massif* of Pen-y-Ghent, 2,231ft above sea level, dominates the background, on the other side of the infant River Ribble.

Here are two more views on the scenic Settle & Carlisle line.

Above: After climbing mightily from Settle to Blea Moor, the running is generally level for 10 miles in the High Pennines until Ais Gill is reached. At the halfway point along this section, south of Garsdale station, the Midland Railway was bold enough to insert water troughs to allow through trains to pick up water 'on the hoof'. Here BR Standard Class 5 4-6-0 No 73158 of Patricroft depot, Manchester, has gained enough speed with its fitted van freight to pick up water on Saturday, 19 August 1967.

Below: In earlier years, fitted freights were commonly in the hands of 'Crab' 2-6-0s, such as No 42751 of Carlisle Kingmoor depot, just starting to nose downhill from Ais Gill summit on the pleasant afternoon of Thursday, 17 August 1961. Ahead lies 47 miles of predominantly downhill running to the outskirts of Carlisle, much of it at 1 in 100. Ais Gill, summit of the line at 1,167ft above sea level, is adjacent to some marshy ground which is the source of the rivers Eden and Ure.

CARLISLE APPROACHES

At last, we arrive at Carlisle, west coast gateway to Scotland. Railways first reached here in 1836 (from the east), and before the Grouping of 1923, seven companies used the joint station, termed 'Citadel' for many years. Four of the companies were English: the London & North Western, Midland, North Eastern and Maryport & Carlisle Railways. Three were Scottish: the Caledonian, Glasgow & South Western and North British Railways. Each had a different livery for locomotives and coaches; this kaleidoscope of colour under one station roof forms an image that many railway enthusiasts would be keen to re-create if they possessed a time machine.

After 1923, the companies were amalgamated to form just two, the LMS and the LNER. Carlisle remained a popular place, where the largest locomotives of the two companies, the products of Stanier, Gresley, Ivatt, Peppercorn, Fowler and Thompson, and later still the Riddles-designed BR Standard engines, rubbed shoulder-to-shoulder. This 'show' caused the late Eric Treacy, doyen of British Railway photographers, to memorably describe Carlisle as the 'giants' rendezvous'.

Below: Towards the end of steam, most of the regular work performed by four-cylinder and three-cylinder locomotives was in the hands of Type 4 diesels – which were not always so powerful or reliable. But at certain times, particularly summer Saturdays and bank holidays, the simpler and rugged 'Black Fives' came into their own, with more than 100 examples still in service in the last couple of years, mostly in North West England. On Saturday, 17 July 1965, No 45027 of Carnforth sets out from Carlisle with a southbound train. Already the tracks to Carlisle goods depot (site of the original passenger terminus), across the Settle & Carlisle line bridge in the right background, have been removed.

Bottom: Ivatt Class 2 2-6-2 tank No 41222 of Upperby shunts at the south end of Carlisle station, on 17 July 1965. These engines replaced the Class 3F 'Jinty' 0-6-0 tanks earlier in that year. No 41222's early career was spent nearly 300 miles south of Carlisle; in 1955 it was involved in a serious firebox blowback and runaway incident on the Luton to Dunstable branch.

Above: Here is some evidence that Carlisle was indeed the 'giants' rendezvous'! On Saturday, 7 August 1965, 'Black Five' No 45069 of Liverpool Edge Hill depot is pulling out from Platform 4 with the Glasgow to Liverpool train. 'Jubilee' No 45697 *Arethusa* of Leeds Holbeck awaits 1M97 the 12.40 Gourock to Leicester and No 72006 *Clan Mackenzie* of Carlisle Kingmoor waits for the rush to clear before backing down on to the 16.25 all stations to Bradford Forster Square local train.

Left: Carlisle will be forever associated with the Stanier 'Duchess' Pacifics, or 'big uns' as they were affectionately referred to by enginemen. Here is one of the massive 161-ton machines, Crewe North's No 46246 *City of Manchester* at the north end of Platform 3. It is being watered for the journey through from Crewe to Scotland on Tuesday, 7 June 1960, and will take its leave of London Midland Region territory at Gretna Junction, eight miles north of Carlisle, in a few minutes' time.

It was inevitable that the steam era would come to an end, and the signs were highlighted, even to the general public, by vast quantities of disused steam engines congregating at depots and sidings throughout Britain.

This volume does not delve into the melancholy cutting-up operations at works and scrapyards. These two views will suffice to remind us of steam's impending demise, accompanied by the gloom felt so strongly by most railway enthusiasts.

Above: These two Stanier Class 2P 0-4-4 tanks (there was not much 'Stanier' about them, apart from the rear bogie truck) were stored for some three years at both Rugby and Coventry depots, having been displaced from local work on the Leamington-Coventry-Nuneaton route. Nos 41909 and 41902 are seen outside the disused Rugby Locomotive Works on Sunday, 8 November 1959. It was early 1962 before they reached Cashmore's of Great Bridge for cutting up. Five years later, the pair would have been certain preservation candidates.

Right: An 'old favourite' for many was the Midland Class 2F 0-6-0 from Burton-on-Trent, No 58186. Neilson-built in 1876, it ended its days very visibly, being cut up by the local contractor, Bridges, in Water Orton goods yard. The engine is here shown near its last resting-place on Saturday, 4 August 1962. In the background is Water Orton marshalling yard, full of four-wheeled wagons of all descriptions. Centre stage is occupied by a Cravens-built three-car DMU which is leaving Water Orton station on a Derby or Leicester to Birmingham New Street working; this train would survive into the era when steam traction, and most wagonload traffic, was gone from our railways. These might have been economical moves, but they heralded a much less interesting era for railway watchers!